DESPERATE HOUSEWIVES

BEHIND CLOSED DOORS

This book is dedicated to
Martha Cherry,

*'The Original
Desperate Housewife'*

DESPERATE
HOUSEWIVES

BEHIND CLOSED DOORS

DESIGNED BY

Number Seventeen, NYC

PRODUCED BY

Downtown
Bookworks Inc.

CONTENTS

The **INTRODUCTION**

In April of 2002 I was absolutely "desperate." I was broke, unable to get even an interview for a writing job, and seriously concerned about my future. I had just turned forty and was starting to wonder if I was one of those deluded writers that wander around Hollywood, convincing themselves they're talented when all the evidence points to the contrary. But, because I have a lot of self-esteem (absolutely the result of parents who adored me) I started writing the first draft of Desperate Housewives *convinced it would turn things around.*

Boy, was I right! In fact, the reality completely exceeded my fantasies. And that's remarkable given that I can dream pretty big.

As I write this, it's May of 2005 and I'm sitting in a gorgeous hotel suite in London enjoying an all-too-brief holiday before work begins on the second season of DH. I've read every page of this wonderful book chronicling our first season, and I'm struck by the amazing journey my characters have taken over the past year. The way their lives have grown and changed with hilarious and, occasionally, heartbreaking results. A big thank you goes out to my talented actors, directors, and writing staff who made it all happen.

I'm also struck by the fact that Susan, Lynette, Bree, and Gabrielle are no longer exclusively mine. They now belong not only to my aforementioned co-workers, but to millions of fans around the world who feel they know them as well as I do. It's an odd feeling. But it makes me happy. And proud.

In fact, things are going so well, I'm almost able to forget what it was like to be desperate.

Almost.

Luckily, memories of the uncertainty and fear I had in 2002 will stay with me for the rest of my life. And thank God for that. How else would I be able to write Season Two of Desperate Housewives without them?

Enjoy the book. Keep watching the series. And a big thank you.

Marc Cherry

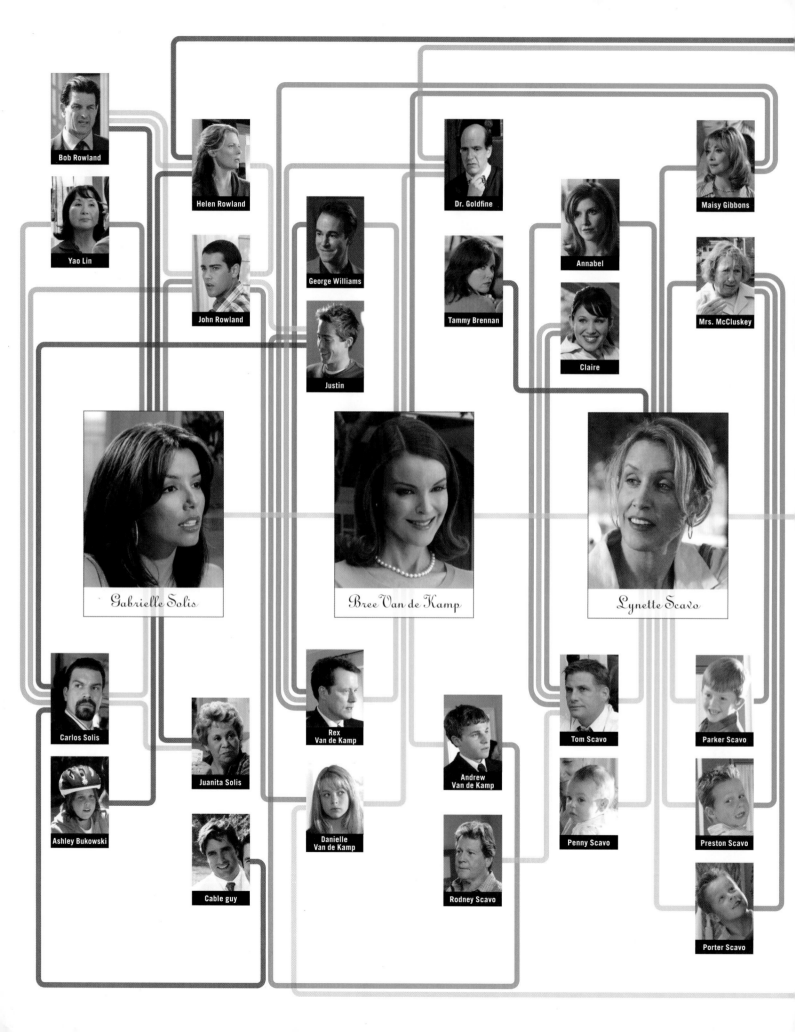

Bob Rowland

Yao Lin

Helen Rowland

John Rowland

George Williams

Justin

Dr. Goldfine

Tammy Brennan

Annabel

Claire

Maisy Gibbons

Mrs. McCluskey

Gabrielle Solis

Bree Van de Kamp

Lynette Scavo

Carlos Solis

Juanita Solis

Ashley Bukowski

Cable guy

Rex Van de Kamp

Danielle Van de Kamp

Andrew Van de Kamp

Rodney Scavo

Tom Scavo

Penny Scavo

Parker Scavo

Preston Scavo

Porter Scavo

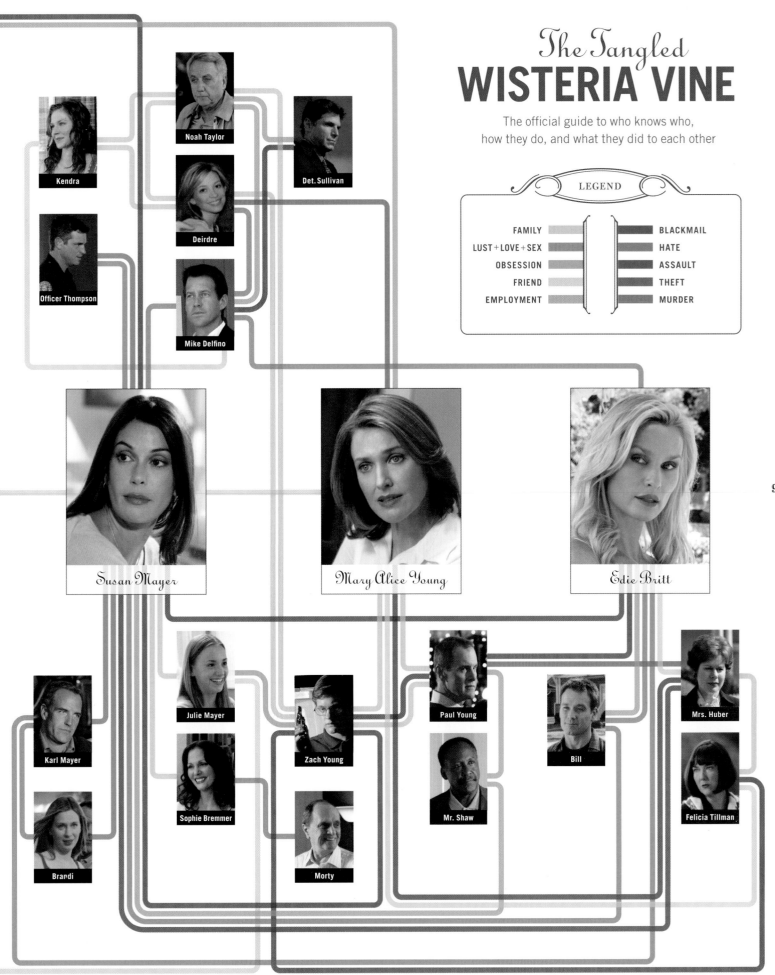

The Tangled
WISTERIA VINE
The official guide to who knows who,
how they do, and what they did to each other

LEGEND

FAMILY	BLACKMAIL
LUST + LOVE + SEX	HATE
OBSESSION	ASSAULT
FRIEND	THEFT
EMPLOYMENT	MURDER

Kendra

Noah Taylor

Det. Sullivan

Deirdre

Officer Thompson

Mike Delfino

Susan Mayer

Mary Alice Young

Edie Britt

9

Karl Mayer

Brandi

Julie Mayer

Sophie Bremmer

Zach Young

Morty

Paul Young

Mr. Shaw

Bill

Mrs. Huber

Felicia Tillman

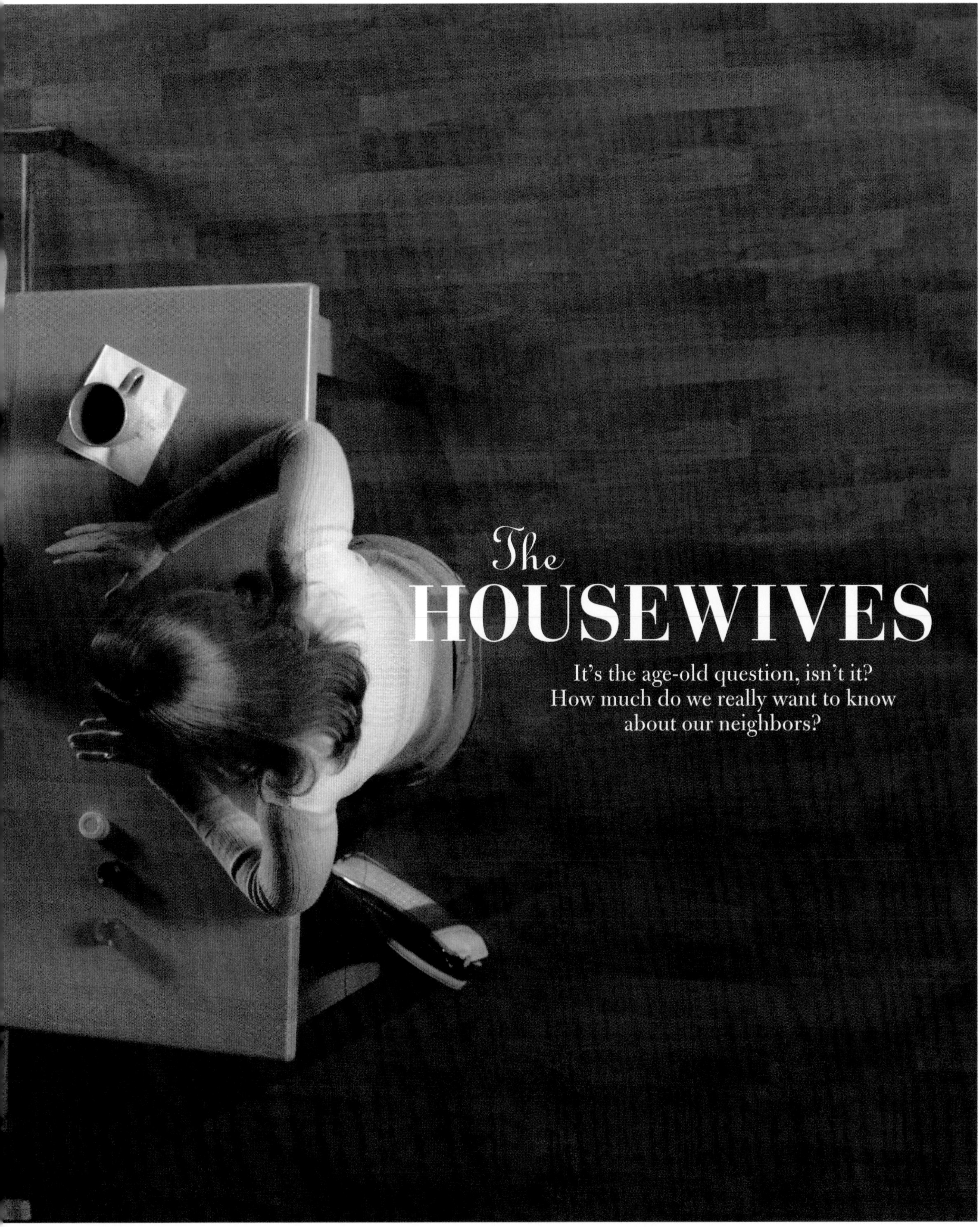

The HOUSEWIVES

It's the age-old question, isn't it?
How much do we really want to know
about our neighbors?

"IN TRUTH, I SPENT THE DAY AS I SPENT EVERY OTHER DAY, QUIETLY POLISHING THE ROUTINE OF MY LIFE UNTIL IT GLEAMED WITH PERFECTION. THAT'S WHY IT WAS SO ASTONISHING WHEN I DECIDED TO GO TO MY HALLWAY CLOSET AND RETRIEVE A REVOLVER THAT HAD NEVER BEEN USED."

Mysterious
MARY ALICE YOUNG

THE CENTER THAT FELL OUT

Mary Alice's APHORISMS

An odd thing happens when we die. Our senses vanish. Taste, touch, smell, and sound become a distant memory. But our sight, ah, our sight expands, and we can suddenly see the world we've left behind so clearly. Of course, most of what's visible to the dead could also be seen by the living. If they'd only take the time to look.

After I died, I began to surrender the parts of myself that were no longer necessary. My desires, beliefs, ambitions, doubts; every trace of my humanity was discarded. I discovered when moving through eternity, it helps to travel lightly. In fact, I held onto only one thing: my memory.

Suburbia is a battle-ground, an arena for all forms of domestic combat. Husbands clash with wives, parents cross swords with children. But the bloodiest battles often involve women and their mothers-in-law.

Most mothers will tell you that children are a gift from God. Most mothers will also tell you there are some days when you wish you could return them.

Mary Alice is the most mysterious of the housewives because we only know bits and pieces of her story. A loving, doting wife and mother who was generous to her friends, she was the last person any of them would have expected to shoot herself in the head.

In death, Mary Alice sees things she would not have seen in life: her friends' vulnerabilities, lies, and secrets. She doesn't judge them so much as love them more because of their foibles, pitying them for the ways they manipulate and hurt those they care about most.

Perhaps because Mary Alice represents a part of them, the women decide to get to the bottom of her suicide. They can't quite make sense of why her husband and son are so odd, or why this vivacious woman has married a man who seems to be withholding and cold.

After finding a blackmail note in Mary Alice's clothes, the women make a series of discoveries: She was being treated by Dr. Goldfine; she once went by another name, Angela; and she may have had something to do with a disappeared baby. When Felicia Tillman comes to town and realizes she knew Mary Alice by her former identity, it's only a matter of time before the women learn just how much Mary Alice may have been hiding.

BIRTHDAY
MARCH 25

HOMETOWN
PORTLAND, OREGON

A familiar face on television, Strong has guest starred on the CBS hit *CSI* and recurred on the FX Network's popular *Nip/Tuck*, *Everwood* on the WB, and on the critically acclaimed Aaron Sorkin series *Sports Night* on ABC. She is also recognizable to *Seinfeld* fans as Sue Ellen Mishkie, better known as "The Braless Wonder."

Strong stars in the upcoming features *The Kid and I* with Tom Arnold and *The Work and the Glory*. Previous film credits include *Starship Troopers*, *Starship Troopers 2*, *The Deep End of the Ocean* with Michelle Pfeiffer and Treat Williams, *The Craft*, and the Mel Brooks classic *Spaceballs*.

13

Strong is a certified yoga instructor with her own studio in Los Angeles and she has a line of videos designed to help infertile couples through yoga therapy. She has also taught at UCLA's Mind-Body Institute.

She lives in Los Angeles with her husband and son.

an interview with
BRENDA STRONG

When I sat down to do the scene during the pilot where all of us console Susan, an image came to me. That image was that Mary Alice Young was the hub of a wheel, and all of them were spokes, and when that center point fell out, all the spokes just went spinning without any grounding. She was an extremely grounding force. And that's what was so difficult for every character to imagine: How could someone who was so loving and so grounded do this? It's like the picture on a TV dinner package that makes the food look really good, but then you open the cover, and those mashed potatoes and peas are not what they seem.

I teach yoga—it's one of my true loves—and I've had students come up after class and say, "I'm so sorry, but when you were guiding that meditation, all I could think about was Mary Alice because you sounded so much like you do on the show."

Sometimes I find Mary Alice's voice coming out of me. It's mostly at night when I lay down with my son and read him stories. That's really what Mary Alice is: a storyteller.

Surprising

SUSAN MAYER

**THE
CALAMITY
JANE
OF WISTERIA
LANE**

I knew Susan was going to be my anchor character, and I didn't really know my take on her at first. And then it occurred to me that one of these women should be divorced. The others are desperate in their fairy-tale lives and Susan is a single mom with a kid whose first fairy-tale life exploded, and now she wants back in. I thought there was something so real about a woman saying, "I don't have much time left," and when this available hunky guy moves onto the street, something in her saying "Let me at him." — Marc Cherry

THE SONG SUSAN SINGS WHILE SHE'S GETTING READY FOR HER ROMANTIC INTERLUDE
WITH MIKE IS THE AL GREEN CLASSIC "HERE I AM (COME AND TAKE ME)."

Susan's best quality is also the one that gets her into the most trouble: her huge, open heart. Vivacious, smart, and warm, Susan has a habit of opening herself too easily and seeing the best in everyone, even when her judgment tells her otherwise. And though she would love to be poised and confident, she has a bad habit of falling on her face at inopportune moments — she smashed into a cake at a wedding and nearly got devoured Tippi Hedren–style by a crazed bird. Then there was the time she wound up naked in the middle of Wisteria Lane, with nowhere to hide, only to be discovered by neighborhood heartthrob Mike Delfino.

SUSAN
I'm trying a new strategy. I'm playing hard to get.

JULIE
How long do you think you can keep that up?

SUSAN
Oh, maybe until noon. Then I'm going to have to run over there and beg him to love me.

LYNETTE
Did you bat your eyes? You know, it doesn't work if you don't bat your eyes.

SUSAN
Honey, I batted everything that wasn't nailed down. I'm telling you—nothin'.

JULIE
No man has seen you naked in years. Except your doctor.

SUSAN
And he retired. I try not to take that personally.

SUSAN
Okay, I know this sounds weird, but I just need to have my things around me.

MIKE
What things?

SUSAN
Perfumes, and oils … and I want to pick out the outfit that you're going to tear off me.

SUSAN
I don't hate Zach. I just think he's sort of crazy.

JULIE
Mom, I've heard people call you sort of crazy.

SUSAN
Well, I'm adorable crazy. And he's … rampage crazy.

16

At Mary Alice's wake, Susan is still emotionally raw from her divorce one year earlier from her rake of a husband, Karl. A children's book illustrator, Susan would go to the ends of the earth for her daughter, Julie — her friend, her confidante, the person she trusts with (almost) all her secrets. In fact, sometimes Susan's need for Julie is so strong that it's hard to tell who's the mother and who's the daughter. After Susan lays eyes on a handsome plumber, Mike, at the wake, she sets her sights on him — only to be thwarted by Edie Britt at nearly every turn.

Susan loves strongly and sometimes too hard; hopefully Mike will be gentle with her and not wound her the way Karl did.

"I GUESS I DO INVITE THE DRAMA IN."

Though she is a die-hard romantic, Susan is also brainy, crafty, and strong-willed. She has no problem telling Mrs. Huber just what she thinks of her, or giving Zach Young a talking-to, or lecturing Gabrielle when she learns she is having an extramarital affair.

It is this same inner vitality that makes her determined to get to the bottom of Mary Alice's suicide. As she does a little sleuthing, she begins to suspect that Paul Young has done something bad. Then she discovers that Julie has struck up an intimate friendship with Mary Alice's odd son, Zach. When Susan catches Zach and Julie kissing, she bans Julie from seeing him. For the first time, the mother and daughter who were best friends find themselves straining to get along.

"I'm mad because I like you so much without really knowing anything about you."

Macaroni & Cheese

{ if only Susan knew this recipe }

MAKES 8 SERVINGS

4 tablespoons	**Salt and pepper**
UNSALTED BUTTER, PLUS MORE FOR CASSEROLE DISH	TO TASTE
8 ounces (2 cups)	**½ teaspoon**
ELBOW MACARONI	DRY MUSTARD
¾ cup	**Pinch**
PANKO (JAPANESE BREAD CRUMBS)	CAYENNE PEPPER
1 small	**1½ cups**
ONION, MINCED	MILK
2 tablespoons	**2 cups**
ALL-PURPOSE FLOUR	SHREDDED SHARP CHEDDAR CHEESE

1 ~ Heat oven to 350°F. Butter a 2-quart casserole dish; set aside. ~ 2 ~ In a large saucepot over high heat, bring 4 quarts of water to boil. Add salt and the macaroni. Cook until just al dente, 8 to 10 minutes. Drain well. ~ 3 ~ In a small saucepan over medium heat, melt 2 tablespoons butter. Remove from heat and stir in breadcrumbs. Set aside. ~ 4 ~ In a medium saucepan over medium heat, melt remaining 2 tablespoons butter. Add onions and cook until translucent. Stir in flour, mustard, and cayenne. Season with salt and pepper. Gradually stir in milk and continue stirring until sauce is thickened. Remove pan from heat and stir in cheese. ~ 5 ~ Pour macaroni into prepared casserole dish. Pour cheese sauce over macaroni and stir until combined. Sprinkle with panko mixture. ~ 6 ~ Bake until top is golden, and sauce bubbles around the edges, 20 to 30 minutes. Transfer dish to a wire rack and let cool for 5 minutes before serving.

"This dress is riding up as it is. If I walk any faster, it's going to be Happy Valentine's Day for everyone"

As her relationship with Mike heats up, Susan begins to soften, happy in the glow of a guy who cares about her so much he even said "I love you" first. But after Mike is arrested for Mrs. Huber's murder, Susan learns that he's a former drug dealer who's been convicted of manslaughter. Hurt and angry, she breaks up with him, only to sink into a miserable depression. She doesn't want to trust him, or any man, again — and what woman hasn't been there? The lovebirds reconcile, but Susan's nosy nature plants her in Mike's house with Zach Young holding her at gunpoint. Mike has already saved her heart — but can he save her life?

Dressing Susan

KLUTZY, ARTISTIC, A LITTLE BIT TWISTED

Susan is known for being artistic and sometimes uncoordinated, and these are traits that both actress Teri Hatcher and costume designer Catherine Adair try to reflect in her clothes. "Susan is a single mom," says Adair, "and an artist, and Marc's written that she tends to be a little klutzy. So when we thought about the clothes, Teri and I sat down and went to an artistic base.

special occasions — and it is in these scenes that Adair gets to show off Hatcher's figure and her great sense of comedy. "Teri's physical comedy is so good and so you want to play with it. Teri can take a short skirt and make it even shorter. She knows how to move and work it." Hence, the charity fashion-show scene, in which Susan stumbled onto the catwalk

We go for the feeling that she's fallen in love with a belt from a swap meet that she wears with a T-shirt that's three years old and a hot new pair of pants that she just bought before she picked her daughter up from school. I wanted a feeling of mix-and-match, just a little eccentric, but not so kooky that you'd look at the clothes instead of watching the character."

In keeping with her character, we often see Susan in thermal-style shirts, corduroy pants, or jeans, or layered tops, with eye-catching jewelry. But Susan has another mode too — when she's dressed up for

dressed in almost nothing, and the Valentine's Day scene, in which her dress was so high it was almost "Happy Valentine's Day" to everyone.

Though Adair tries to give Susan an inner sense of style, when she finds an outfit that looks too good on Hatcher, she tends to change it. "The fun with Teri is we'll put an outfit together and then we'll both look and say, 'Mmm, it's a little too together. What can we do to put it into a little bit of disarray? How do you twist it a little bit?'"

BIRTHDAY

DECEMBER 8

HOMETOWN

SUNNYVALE, CALIFORNIA

an interview with
TERI HATCHER

20

I wrote the part of Susan for Mary-Louise Parker. I was a huge fan of her work on The West Wing. *When she turned it down we were able to proceed with auditions. We had major names coming in and reading, and a lot of people were good, but none of them really nailed it. But each time Teri auditioned she got better and better, to the point where her network audition was just one of those glorious experiences where she could do no wrong. She owned the part from that moment on.* — Marc Cherry

Teri Hatcher earned a 2005 Golden Globe Award as "Best Actress in a Leading Role, Musical or Comedy, Television," and a Screen Actors Guild Award for "Outstanding Performance by a Female Actor in a Comedy Series" for her role as Susan Mayer. Like Susan, Hatcher is also a single mom to her young daughter, Emerson.

Best known for her role as Lois Lane in the 1994–97 series *Lois & Clark,* she played Sally Bowles in the national tour of the Tony Award–winning musical *Cabaret* and has toured the globe in Eve Ensler's *The Vagina Monologues*. Film roles include *The Big Picture* directed by Christopher Guest, *Soapdish, Two Days in the Valley, Spy Kids,* and *Tomorrow Never Dies* opposite Pierce Brosnan.

Her first television series was *MacGyver,* and she also appeared on *The Love Boat, LA Law,* and *Murphy Brown.* She played a memorable guest role on *Seinfeld,* uttering the now-famous line, "They're real — and they're spectacular."

Hatcher has topped Best Dressed lists around the world and was voted E! Entertainment Television's "Best Dressed Woman of 1996." She had the distinction of being the most downloaded image on the Internet the year she posed wrapped in Superman's cape — and nothing else.

She was honored with the 1996 "Spirit of Compassion" Award for her generous support of the Aviva Center, which provides services to sexually and physically abused adolescents. She has been a strong supporter of the AIDS Walk in Los Angeles and New York and is active in the battle against breast cancer.

COMEDY IS LIKE DANCING

For an actress, Susan as a character is a gift sent from the heavens. I love Susan and her journey and feel that this is the best part I have ever had, bar none. Susan is a great representation of what each of us deals with daily. Our responsibilities can be overwhelming and things often don't go quite as you planned, so you have to roll with it. Susan celebrates rolling with it.

The physical comedy I get to do with this role is fun. Comedy is like dancing: I choreograph it in my mind and do it over and over again. It's hard for me to watch my own work, but I remember watching the scene where I get stuck naked outside and laughing at the comedy of it all. Who hasn't been locked out? Maybe not all of us were naked, but it's one of those bumps in life we deal with.

LANDING SUSAN

I read the pilot while I was enjoying a fun girls' week-end in Arizona. When I finished, I called my manager, Eli, and said, "This is the best thing I have ever read. I've got to play Susan! I'll just serve coffee on the set, if it means a chance to work with a brilliant writer!" And here we are today.

It was a long audition process, but I was happy to read for as many executives as it took to convince them of my ability to play Susan. Before I left my home for the last audition that day, my daughter called out to me and asked me what I was going to do. I told her I was trying to get a job so we could buy a pony. She said, "Go Mommy!" I arrived at Disney, signed my contract before entering the room and looked out from the 20th-floor window. I felt really peaceful, like all I could do was give the part my best and hopefully everything would work out.

It's amazing that in a year, I went from offering to serve coffee on the set to winning a Golden Globe for my work on the show. I was honored, surprised, and humbled that night.

A GLASS OF CABERNET

The majority of the time I am working with Jamie, Nicollette, and Andrea, all of whom I adore. Jamie is a joy to work with—he is so honest and subtle and he's a great listener. Andrea has so much to give the world artistically—she is as professional as it gets, so her parents must be doing all the right things. And in a world filled with half-truths and shams, I appreciate Nicollette's gift of truthfulness. She owns herself and her role and her confidence is inspiring to me.

Besides the actors, I am really lucky to work with such a supportive crew. It makes all the difference in the world for an actress to work with people who support you.

I think the show works because it's fresh, smart, and easy to watch. The writing is genius. We all want to be entertained—especially after the kids are in bed. It's nice to have something on TV to enjoy with a glass of cabernet.

A GO-GETTER
WHOSE LIFE
TOOK AN
UNEXPECTED
TURN

Lively

LYNETTE SCAVO

"SHE USED TO SEE HERSELF AS A CAREER WOMAN, AND A HUGELY SUCCESSFUL ONE
AT THAT. SHE WAS KNOWN FOR HER POWER LUNCHES, HER EYE-CATCHING
PRESENTATIONS, AND HER RUTHLESSNESS IN WIPING OUT THE COMPETITION.
BUT LYNETTE GAVE UP HER CAREER TO ASSUME A NEW LABEL: THE INCREDIBLY
SATISFYING ROLE OF FULL-TIME MOTHER. UNFORTUNATELY FOR LYNETTE,
THIS NEW LABEL FREQUENTLY FELL SHORT OF WHAT WAS ADVERTISED."

I came up with the character of Lynette first. I wanted to write a career woman who had given up her career so she could raise kids because she wanted to do right by them, and now she's not happy. I thought that was, in its own little way, groundbreaking. In America we make it seem like to be a stay-at-home mom must be so fulfilling. For a woman to say, "No, this is hard, and I don't really like it," I thought that was a brave choice. To make sure that the audience sympathized with Lynette, I made her kids complete nightmares and her husband always away on business. I wanted to say something about how, as much as we revere those roles of wife and mother, it can be a lonely and exasperating life. —Marc Cherry

Lynette's LINGO

EDIE
This is an old-lady dress. You won't even be able to see my body.

LYNETTE
That is so like you, Edie. You're always thinking of others.

23

LYNETTE
You know, our mothers were smart. They didn't get us nannies or put us in day care because they knew if they did, we'd find out there are other women out there who are better mothers than they were.

BREE
Stealing a family's nanny is so... unseemly.

LYNETTE
I'm not twisting anyone's arm. If I make a better offer, why shouldn't a qualified person reap the benefits? So come on — where can I score some high-grade nanny?

LYNETTE
You're not your father.
And just so we're
absolutely clear,
I am definitely not
your mother.
Because if you ever
betray me, I will leave
you. I will take the
kids, and I will walk
out the door and you
will never see any of
us again. Whew. Glad to
get that off my chest.

BREE
You want me to
recommend the twins?

LYNETTE
Yes. You can tell them
how beautifully
well-behaved the
boys are.

BREE
So you want me to lie?

LYNETTE
Yeah. I thought that was
understood.

Lynette Scavo represents that person inside all of us who just can't seem to hold it together. She is lovable because of her chaotic life, her struggles, and, most important, her ability to be honest about them. How could anyone cope with the family Lynette has? She used to be a high-powered ad exec but now her husband Tom travels almost all the time and her ADD-afflicted boys and infant baby are driving her crazy. It is as though she took a new job she thought she would love, and now she desperately misses her old one. It's not that she doesn't love her children, but like many women, she doesn't love being a stay-at-home mother.

"Tom, our last version of 'normal' had me popping pills. 'Normal' is a bad, bad plan."

It doesn't help that her children are impossible to handle. But Lynette is so driven that she tries to apply the same go-getter methods she used at work to being a mom. And it doesn't always work. Worse, Tom seems to have no idea how harried she is. He's oblivious to her plight, and his cluelessness only fuels her frustration.

Lynette is fearless and able to say it like it is. When the world's scariest stay-at-home mother, Maisy Gibbons, insists on a politically correct production of *Little Red Riding Hood,* the irrepressible Lynette gives Maisy a talking-to, even offering to "throw down" outside. But Lynette, though a toughie, is also an intense overachiever, and in her frenzied attempt to get the costumes made on time, she winds up getting hooked on her sons' ADD medication. The career woman who once had it all begins to unravel, realizing she's not cut out for the life she leads.

BREE
So what are you saying?
That the twins
murdered Martha?

LYNETTE
I wouldn't put it
past them.

"I DIDN'T COMPLAIN... THE ENTIRE TIME."

SCAVO FAMILY
FRIED CHICKEN

[Lynette would make it if she only had the time]

— MAKES 4 SERVINGS —

1 QUART
BUTTERMILK

3 TABLESPOONS
KOSHER SALT

1 TABLESPOON
TABASCO® SAUCE

1 (3-TO 4- POUND)
**CHICKEN,
CUT INTO 8 PIECES**

3
EGGS

1 TEASPOON
**FRESHLY GROUND
BLACK PEPPER**

1½ CUPS
MILK

1¼ CUPS
ALL-PURPOSE FLOUR

1 CUP
BREADCRUMBS

1 TEASPOON
HERBES DE PROVENCE

1 QUART
CANOLA OIL

1 In a casserole dish, stir together buttermilk, 1 tablespoon salt, and Tabasco. Add chicken pieces, and turn to coat. Let stand at room temperature for least 30 minutes and up to 2 hours.

2 Heat oven to 300°F. Place a wire rack on a baking sheet and place them in the oven. Add enough oil to a cast-iron skillet to come halfway up the sides of skillet and heat over medium-high heat.

3 While oil heats, whisk together eggs and milk in a large bowl. In a large paper bag, combine flour, breadcrumbs, remaining 2 tablespoons salt, pepper, and herbes de provence.

4 When the oil has reached 350°F, remove the thighs from the buttermilk mixture and place in egg mixture. Turn chicken to coat and transfer to paper bag. Fold paper bag over and shake until chicken is thoroughly coated. Remove chicken from bag, shake off excess coating, and fry, turning once, until golden brown, about 8 minutes. Transfer cooked pieces to wire rack in oven to keep warm. Using a slotted spoon, strain out any crumbs of coating in the oil. Repeat with legs, breasts, and wings, transferring pieces to oven as they cook. Serve hot.

Strung out and exhausted, she hallucinates that Mary Alice is offering her a revolver. When she finally comes down, she admits to Bree and Susan, in one of the most moving scenes of the show, that she thinks she's a terrible mother. This admission itself only becomes more painful to Lynette when her friends confess that they too found motherhood challenging. For the first time Lynette realizes that no one has an easy time of motherhood, and she sobs to the girls, "We should tell each other this stuff."

Seeking a solution to their problems, Tom and Lynette hire a nanny, but she turns out to be just a little bit too attractive to keep around. Then, when Tom is offered a lucrative promotion that entails his traveling for work even more, Lynette finds a way to make sure that the offer is retracted.

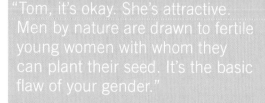

"Tom, it's okay. She's attractive. Men by nature are drawn to fertile young women with whom they can plant their seed. It's the basic flaw of your gender."

Frazzled, but smart and willful, Lynette is a mother and wife who, like many others, wonders how generations of women did it before them. Nostalgic for her old days on the career path, she is ambivalent and frustrated with the challenges of what is supposed to be a placid, ideal life. As she begins to see that what's right for her family might not be right for her, Lynette displays mettle we haven't seen before. When Tom quits his job and decides to be a stay-at-home dad, Lynette is torn by the desire to return to work and anxiety about leaving her kids.

Dressing Lynette

CORPORATE EXECUTIVE, STAY-AT-HOME MOM & PRIVATE SCHOOL PARENT

Adair dresses Lynette according to the three different worlds in which she treads: corporate exec (her former life), stay-at-home mom, and ell-dressed private school mom. "In her previous world," says Adair, "she was a high-powered executive, she wasn't married, she knew how to dress, she knew how to win the deals, and she was invincible. We get glimpses of that when she

about comfort and the fact that by the time she's got everybody else ready in the day she doesn't have time for herself." For mother mode, Lynette wears a lot of J. Crew, frequently borrowing shirts that we've seen Tom wearing in other scenes.

The third world is the one that emerged in the second half of Season One: the more high-pressure world of a prestigious private school.

has to dress up." For this mode, Adair uses designers like Armani, Malone, and Dolce & Gabbana. "When you think of Dolce & Gabbana," Adair points out, "you think of the flashier, more flamboyant things, but they also cut beautifully tailored, very simple-looking suits."

Adair calls the second world "private mom": that of an overwhelmed mother who doesn't have time to put outfits together. "Because Felicity is such a conscientious actress and because she is also a mother in real life, she pays great attention to detail— we'll put baby food on clothes, and stains, and make them look crumpled and rumpled. It's all

"She's trying to find a way to fit in," says Adair. "That tends to be skirts and cardigans, things that are looking more safe, but still practical in terms of putting them on. She'll still slip into her Taryn Rose slides." For public mom, Adair makes many of the skirts herself, and also uses Three Dot and simple Anthropologie pieces.

Though we seldom get to see Lynette in dressy clothing, Adair says she enjoys it when she can glam Huffman up. "Felicity has an amazing body. When we show her off, I really go to the nines, because she's just flawless."

Felicity came in and wowed us so much that we knew it was her part. Within fifteen minutes she had the part. We were very lucky there. —Marc Cherry

an interview with
FELICITY HUFFMAN

BIRTHDAY
DECEMBER 9
HOMETOWN
BEDFORD, NEW YORK

Huffman has appeared in the feature films *Christmas with the Kranks, Raising Helen,* and the independent film *Transamerica,* which screened at the 2005 Tribeca Film Festival, where she took home Best Actress honors. On the small screen she appeared in the television movie *Reversible Errors* with William H. Macy, Tom Selleck, and Monica Potter.

Among her other television movie credits are *Out of Order,* the critically-acclaimed *Door to Door* starring William H. Macy, *Path to War* with Alec Baldwin and Donald Sutherland. She has appeared on the shows *Chicago Hope, X-Files, Law & Order, Bedtime Stories,* and was a series regular on *The Human Factor, Sports Night, Thunder Alley, Early Edition, Jules,* and *The Golden Years.*

Huffman is a founding member of the Atlantic Theater Company, an off-Broadway theater company where she has appeared in numerous plays such as *Dangerous Corner, Shaker Heights,* and *The Joy of Definitely Going Somewhere.* She also appeared in David Mamet's *Speed the Plow* and received an Obie award for her portrayal of Donnie in Mamet's *Cryptogram.*

Huffman resides in Los Angeles with her husband, actor/director William H. Macy.

THE DRUMS GO OUT

Every pilot season, there are a couple of pilots, usually, God willing, that make the drums go out. And there's word out, "You've got to read the pilot, you've got to read the pilot." I read the pilot and I thought it was great. What appeals to me is good writing because it's easy to act, it makes you look good, and it's truthful.

I went in on it at six o'clock at night, which is a bad time for my children, because they're in the bath and they don't want me to leave. It was raining out and my kids were screaming. So I tried to pull myself together in this cute, "Look at me, I'm so together" thing. I went in and when I showed up, I was cranky. I said, "I had to put my kids down and this is hard and I'm grumpy." And I later found out that I'd looked like a wreck. And then I got the job. I truly think it was because I looked like a wreck and was tired and cranky. You never know.

In the audition I said, "I'm so glad you wrote this part. I've been allergic to playing mothers or wives in the past because they're boring." And when I read it and saw that what was up for Lynette was the monumental difficulty of motherhood and all that that entails, losing herself and trying to raise her children and trying to do a good job, I really appreciated it. I don't know how Marc did it.

MODERN MOTHERHOOD

I was in a meeting once with these older women whose children were grown and my oldest daughter was one at that point. After the meeting, we sat back and were chitchatting and they went, "Don't you just love being a mom?" And it was out of my mouth before I could stop it. I said, "No." And they looked at me like I was a criminal. I was so aghast at their reaction and that I had let out my deep, dark secret that I got in the car and sobbed. I had to pull over to the side of the road and call my husband and just sob on the phone for fifteen minutes. I was saying, "I made a mistake, I shouldn't be a mother. How could I say that?"

I find motherhood incredibly difficult, and I know not all women do and God bless them. But I think there is an unspoken pressure between women. My friend was talking about her two-year-old and she said, "Oh, I just hate giving her a bath every night." It's because it's the end of the day and you're out of juice and you just can't do one more thing. You just want to sit down. But she immediately felt that she had to follow that up with, "Oh, but she's so fantastic and I love her so much." You're not allowed to say, "I don't like this right now," the way you could about your spouse or your best friend or your job. It enrages me. I mean, children are difficult enough without robbing women of their true experience of it.

ACTION DEFINES CHARACTER

The logistics of Lynette's character are different than the logistics in my life. Action defines character, and what Lynette has to do is stay home, with her husband away, with three boys and one girl under the age of seven. That, in and of itself, is a host of difficulties and challenges and insanity that I don't have. I have two children. My husband's home and I have help.

I would ask for help a lot sooner and more often than Lynette. She seems to be very proud of going, "I can do this, I can do this."

Lynette's kids are also written to be really difficult kids. In order to have good drama or good comedy, everything has to be heightened. So Marc has heightened it.

Women have come up to me and said, "Oh, God, I love your character. That was me last night. I have three boys," or "I have one kid." I'm so glad. It's so nice to have company in your experience because motherhood is lonely. And when you're thinking, "I'm losing my mind and I'm doing it wrong," and you see this woman on TV who's alone and losing her mind, you think, *Fantastic. I'm not an alien.*

Breezy
BREE VAN DE KAMP

AN
ORCHID
IN
BLOOM

"I REMEMBER THE EASY CONFIDENCE OF HER SMILE,
THE GENTLE ELEGANCE OF HER HANDS,
THE REFINED WARMTH OF HER VOICE. BUT WHAT I
REMEMBER MOST ABOUT BREE WAS THE LOOK
OF FEAR IN HER EYES. BREE HAD STARTED TO REALIZE
HER WORLD WAS UNRAVELING.
AND FOR A WOMAN WHO DESPISED LOOSE ENDS,
THAT WAS UNACCEPTABLE."

Bree's
BARBS

BREE
The least I could do was make sure you boys had a decent meal to look forward to in the morning. I know you're out of your minds with grief.

PAUL
Yes, we are.

BREE
Of course, I will need the baskets back once you're done.

BREE
Hi, Danielle.
How was school?

DANIELLE
It was okay.

BREE
Good.
Where does Andrew keep his marijuana?

31

"Rex cries after he ejaculates."

Bree's desperation starts with the pilot because her husband says he wants a divorce. And this woman whose life is built on this idea of perfection just doesn't understand what's going on. I've had the most fun writing Bree because that's the character that's most like my mom. She wanted everything and everyone to be pleasant. Emotion was frowned upon. We got hugs but there was no yelling in our household. If I had teenage angst I was not allowed to express it. I exaggerate it a little bit in the Van de Kamp household, because there are so many Protestants who, unlike some of the Jewish and Italian families I know, just keep it quiet. — Marc Cherry

Over the course of the season, Bree has suffered perhaps more than any other character, finding her idyllic, plastic existence challenged by a series of new domestic dramas. In each of her travails she surprises the audience in new ways — revealing that she loves sex, is open to S&M, and wants real intimacy, despite seeming incapable of feeling. As her life shifts in strange and unpredictable ways, Bree, like a flower, opens up, becoming warmer, more nuanced, more complex, and real.

REX
We're going to be doing psychological role-play here, Bree, and a funny word like "Boise" will ruin the mood. We need something that sounds serious.

BREE
Hmm. How about "Palestine"?

32

In the pilot, Bree's teenaged children Andrew and Danielle despise her and her husband Rex wants to leave her, saying he just can't live in this "detergent commercial" anymore. He wants the woman he fell in love with, who used to burn the toast and drink the milk out of the carton, and laugh, not this cold, perfect thing she's become. Bree is wounded by his request, so wounded that, whether purposefully or not, she almost poisons him to death. No one messes with Bree, and no one tells her what to do.

"We're WASPs, Dr. Goldfine. Not acknowledging the elephant in the room is what we do best."

Although she wants to have the perfect marriage, she also wants her marriage to work, and showing surprising openness, she suggests they go to couples therapy. It's not long before she learns that Rex cheated on her with Maisy Gibbons. The moralistic, NRA-supporting Bree, who has never once strayed, is so furious at his betrayal that she determines to divorce him. Then she decides instead to opt for revenge, dating the strange loner pharmacist George Williams. Though her motivation was only to hurt Rex, as she gets to know George she discovers that she enjoys his company. In the most unlikely of places she begins to get to know what she wants in a companion, and in a sense, who she really is.

As the Van de Kamps struggle in their marriage, Bree has to deal with two angry children who seem to blame her for all the family's problems. When Andrew confesses that he was involved in a hit-and-run, this devoted mother hides the evidence so Andrew will be off the hook, and then realizes sadly that he doesn't feel at all repentant. The extremely religious, moralistic Bree has birthed a child with no apparent moral compass — and as the truth of that sinks in, Bree wonders if she has failed as a parent.

"My daughter is planning on giving you her virginity and I'd consider it a personal favor if you wouldn't take it."

Bree's Blueberry Muffins

{Perfect every time}

MAKES 12 MUFFINS

3 cups **ALL-PURPOSE FLOUR**	¾ cup & 1 tablespoon **SUGAR**	¼ cup (½ stick) **UNSALTED BUTTER, MELTED AND COOLED SLIGHTLY**
1½ teaspoons **BAKING POWDER**	2 large eggs **LIGHTLY BEATEN**	1 teaspoon **VANILLA EXTRACT**
½ teaspoon **BAKING SODA**	1 cup **BUTTERMILK**	1½ cups **BLUEBERRIES, LIGHTLY COATED WITH ½ CUP FLOUR**
¼ teaspoon **KOSHER SALT**		

1. Heat oven to 350°F.
Grease the cups of a 12-cup muffin pan and line with paper liners.

2. In a large bowl, whisk together the flour, baking powder, baking soda, salt, and ¾ cup sugar.

3. In a 2-cup measuring cup, stir together eggs, buttermilk, and butter. Make a well in the center of the dry ingredients and pour in liquid ingredients. Stir just until mixed, being careful not to overmix (batter may be lumpy). Using a rubber spatula, gently fold in blueberries.

4. Using a #16 ice cream scoop, scoop batter into muffin cups, filling cups two-thirds full. Lightly sprinkle batter with the remaining tablespoon sugar. Bake, rotating pan halfway through baking time, until golden and the tops spring back when pressed lightly, 30 to 33 minutes.

> "All I'm saying is that we're both going to die eventually, and in the time that we have left, whether it's two days or two decades, I think that we should be nice to each other."

Just as she seems to be opening her heart to others, Bree discovers her son Andrew may be gay. No matter how sophisticated she would like to be, she believes homosexuality is a sin and tells the son she loves that he must change.

With her once-perfect family now fractured, Bree encounters a loss more painful than all the others. Rex dies under mysterious circumstances, and Bree becomes a widow. Little does she know that George Williams, the pharmacist and her possible love interest, is the very man who killed him!

"THE LEAST WE CAN DO IS TRY TO KEEP UP APPEARANCES"

34

Despite all the challenges to their relationship, the more Rex and Bree fight the more she realizes the extent of her devotion to him. Bree has been a one-man girl from the moment she met Rex at a Young Republicans meeting. Showing a bravery we might not have expected from her, she finally gets him to admit his secret sexual proclivity: sadomasochistic sex. And the most unlikely dominatrix on the planet, a woman who probably would have been satisfied with the missionary position for life, agrees to role-play with handcuffs (as long as she can run them through the dishwasher first).

But peace for Bree is fleeting, and just as she and Rex seem to be coming together again, she learns that Rex was paying for sex with Maisy. First she tries bribing Maisy so the truth doesn't come out, but when that fails she realizes that there is a better place to spend her money — on a friend in need, Gabrielle — deepening the women's friendship and strengthening their bond.

Dressing Bree

MODERN, STRUCTURED, with TIPS to the '50s

In costuming Bree, Adair uses a lot of structured skirts and pants that show off Marcia Cross' great figure. Though many may think of Bree as a '50s housewife, she rarely dresses in period clothing. Instead Adair tries to do what she calls "tips" to the '50s without making the outfits too stylized. "The secret with Bree," says Adair, "is that her clothes have to look like they're modern. We can

Achieving the Bree look can be tiring—the most time-consuming part of Cross's preparation is maintaining her flip-style haircut. "It's my fault," Cross says. "I picked the haircut." Though she felt the hairstyle was right for the character, she had no idea how time-consuming it would be to maintain it. "In future seasons," says Cross, "I would like to see her

tip to mid-century American style but we'll never dress her in a complete Jackie Kennedy suit." To achieve this look, Adair uses Tahari, Marc Jacobs and Anthropologie and pieces of vintage clothes that she recuts and restructures.

Marcia Cross herself says her personal style is nothing like Bree's. "I'm all about comfort," says Cross, who often switches into terry-cloth slippers between takes. "If it's not comfortable I don't wear it. I'm a flats person and a cargo pants girl whose hair is always in a ponytail. Bree's the opposite. She's all about how it looks."

punched up a little bit, looking a little more Ralph Lauren, as she gets wiser to the ways of the world. It would be nice to see her hair and style change.

I had this feeling of her being stuck in time," says Cross, "and there was something about that hairstyle that recalled a different era, like Smith College in the '50s. Her haircut, values, ideas have not evolved over time."

an interview with
MARCIA CROSS

BIRTHDAY
MARCH 25
HOMETOWN
MARLBOROUGH, MASSACHUSETTS

Marcia Cross was determined to become an actress from the moment she performed in her first school play, *The Witch of Blackbird Pond*, in the sixth grade. At the age of 18 she was accepted at the Juilliard School as a drama major.

On stage, Cross performed in *La Ronde* at the Williamstown Theater Festival, in *Twelfth Night* at the Hartford Stage Company, and in *Two Gentlemen of Verona* at the Old Globe in San Diego.

Her first television job was on the daytime drama *The Edge of Night*. Leaving New York to try her luck in Los Angeles, Cross was soon landing roles in television movies such as *The Last Days of Frank and Jesse James*, costarring with Johnny Cash and Kris Kristofferson.

She is well known from her role as Dr. Kimberly Shaw on the hit drama *Melrose Place*, a role that began when she was hired for one episode. The producers were so impressed, they kept asking her back for additional appearances, eventually bringing her character back from the dead to continue on the hit show.

Cross also guest starred on such series as *Seinfeld*, where she played Jerry's dermatologist girlfriend, and *Cheers*, where she portrayed the younger sister to Kirstie Alley's character. Cross has also appeared on the comedies *Ally McBeal*, *Spin City*, *The Garry Shandling Show* and *King of Queens*. Her dramatic roles include appearances on *CSI*, *Profiler* and *Touched by an Angel*, and she recently starred as Dr. Linda Abbott on the critically acclaimed series *Everwood*. Her film credits include *Living in Fear*, *Always Say Good-bye*, *Dancing in September*, and *Bad Influence*.

Aside from her successful career as an actress, Cross has also made time to continue her education. She recently completed her clinical training to earn a Master's Degree in Psychology.

Marcia's portrayal of Bree has softened so much over the course of the first season. The character has changed tremendously from when I first started with it. You always expect that the actors can take the characters and run with them a little bit. As a writer you have to follow them along and see what they're doing with it. —Marc Cherry

WE BOTH LOVE DEEPLY

I went in and read for Mary Alice, because I'd been flying back and forth doing *Everwood* for a year and I was tired. I thought, *Hmm, I won't have to get made up. I'll be in the background. It'll be a nice gig.* Before I left the room they said, "No, you need to read for Bree." I hadn't even prepared but I jumped right in. And then I got a call that they wanted me to come and test for it.

I thought Bree would be a really hard part to play, and I was right. She's the least like me. Although I use my own heart and soul playing Bree, it's exhausting to be dressed to the nines and perfect every day. I'm messy. I don't try to be perfect. I'm the least domestically inclined of all the actresses. I'll say, "Please teach me how to knit!"

The interesting thing about Bree is that there's what she wants and what she thinks she wants. She thinks she wants everything to be status quo. But actually she wants to be happier.

DUMP HIM!

Fans are generally very happy and complimentary and they love watching her even though she's a little whacked. They make comments about the marriage like, "Dump him!" I thought she'd be the toughest sell so I've been amazed that people do love her. At the beginning people thought she might be an automaton but she has started to change.

Steven is a wonderful Rex. I can't imagine anyone else doing that part. He has been a complete delight and a great, steady partner through all of this. We've had to deal with a lot of dark things. He's a hard worker and he's so committed to Rex and trying to find new colors for him, which is not always that easy. At some point I knew that the key to Bree was loving Rex, no matter what or how he came off. She just loves him and wants his love. It's written in the pilot.

As you go on it gets harder, but in her mind you marry for life. Even with that flirtation with George you know that it's not coming from her heart or her groin. It's, *I'll make him jealous or toy with him a little bit,* not, *I'm going to fall in love.*

AND WE JUST STARTED

In the first few episodes I had to say "scrotum," "ejaculation," and "friction." And I had a scene in my underwear. I thought, *Geez, and we just started.* There's a very free side of her in the safety of the relationship. She is sexual. He's been the one who's more into the fetish aspect of it and hasn't been interested in sex.

I'm looking forward to seeing Bree go through a metamorphosis over the next couple years. I say to the crew, "Breezy Van der Tramp is coming." I'm just aching to get wild and do fun things.

BIRD
IN A
GILDED
CAGE

Glamourous

GABRIELLE SOLIS

I wanted the Solises to be Latino because it was important to me that not all the families on the show be white. Growing up in Southern California, my family had many Mexican families around us and I noticed that in the suburbs, race doesn't matter nearly as much as class. In the neighborhood I was growing up in, no one cared what color you were. They just wanted to make sure that you took care of your lawn. During the writing process, the concept was ordinary housewives. Gabrielle came about because I wanted to make sure there was at least one attractive woman in the cast. I thought, A gorgeous woman goes to the suburbs and she's got all of her material possessions, but she's bored. *And I thought,* If her husband treats her like a trophy wife, what does she do to fill her time? Well, she'll have an affair. — Marc Cherry

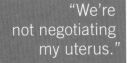

"We're not negotiating my uterus."

39

Gabrielle tends to elicit strong opinions — from her husband Carlos; her teenaged lover, John the gardener; her mother-in-law, Juanita; and not least, her friends. A former runway model in New York, Gabrielle traded in life in the fast lane for her marriage to a rich businessman, after a few years on Wisteria Lane she has begun to realize that, as she puts it so movingly in the pilot episode, "Turns out I wanted all the wrong things."

Gabrielle's GEMS

JOHN
So do you love him?

GABRIELLE
I do.

JOHN
Well, then why are we here? Why are we doing this?

GABRIELLE
Because I don't want to wake up one morning with the sudden urge to blow my brains out.

GABRIELLE
Do you know how bored I was today? I came this close to actually cleaning the house.

GABRIELLE
Good friends support each other after they've been humiliated. Great friends pretend nothing happened in the first place.

40

Caught between a man who adores her (but isn't yet a man) and one who gives her everything except the kind of love she wants, Gabrielle is sinking into despair. She is the woman who has all the material satisfactions anyone could hope for, yet no real joy. Spoiled and provided for, she is lonely, and it is this loneliness that makes her understand Mary Alice's terrible desperation.

Her affair, illicit, sexy, and enviable, is the best thing she has going—but as with anything good, she soon finds herself in danger of having to end it. After Carlos enlists the help of his Madame DeFarge–like mother, Juanita Solis, Gabrielle must connive to keep up her liaisons. As the young lovers become more devious, the emotionally distant Gabrielle learns that John is truly falling in love, forcing her to wonder just what she feels for him in return.

"I've been broke a lot of times in my life. But I've never been poor. Because poor is just a state of mind."

ACTORS RICARDO ANTONIO CHAVIRA AND EVA LONGORIA ARE BOTH FROM TEXAS, BUT THEY DID NOT MEET UNTIL THEY WERE BEING FITTED FOR COSTUMES FOR THE PILOT.

"I WANTED ALL THE WRONG THINGS"

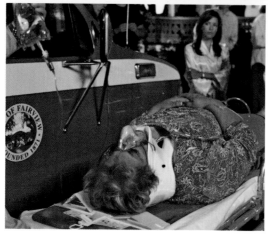

But the hedge trimming grinds to a halt when Juanita photographs Gabrielle and John in the act. As Juanita runs out of the house with her camera, she gets hit by a car. Gabrielle isn't sure whether to feel repentant, or relieved—but her selfish impulses win out and she takes the camera from Juanita's nearly lifeless body. With his mother in a coma, Carlos becomes eager to have children, and announces his desire for family. No matter how guilty she feels about her mother-in-law, Gabrielle is too strong to change her view on parenthood: No kids, ever. As Carlos suggests they negotiate, Gabrielle shouts, "We are not negotiating my uterus!" Little does she know that he has begun replacing her birth control pills with placebos. In the beginning, it was Gabrielle whose moral core seemed questionable, but now her husband's appears to be the one that's lacking.

Spicy Paella

MADE BY YAO LIN

½ cup plus 2 tablespoons
OLIVE OIL

1 cup
DICED HAM

4 links
**CHORIZO,
SLICED INTO 1/2-INCH PIECES**

1 large
ONION, DICED

1 medium
RED BELL PEPPER, DICED

5 cloves
GARLIC, MINCED

6
CHICKEN THIGHS

3 cups
VALENCIA RICE

4 cups
**CHICKEN BROTH,
PLUS MORE AS NEEDED**

1 cup
RED WINE

kosher salt
TO TASTE

¼ teaspoon
CRUMBLED SAFFRON THREADS

1 pound
**LARGE RAW SHRIMP,
PEELED AND DEVEINED**

½ pound
SCALLOPS

1 pound
**CLEANED MONKFISH
(OR COD FILLET)
CUT INTO CUBES**

1 cup
FROZEN GREEN PEAS

2 roasted
**RED PEPPERS,
CUT INTO STRIPS**

¼ cup
**CHOPPED PARSLEY LEAVES,
FOR GARNISH**

Heat oven to 350°F. In a large ovenproof skillet over medium-high heat, heat 2 tablespoons olive oil. Add the ham and chorizo and saute until browned, about 8 minutes. Use a slotted spoon to remove from pan and set aside. Add onions, red pepper, and garlic to pan, and saute just until onion is translucent but not yet golden, about 3 minutes. Add 2 tablespoons of oil and the chicken pieces skin-side down. Cook, turning once, until browned on both sides, about 15 minutes. Remove chicken from pan and set aside.

Reduce heat to medium and add 2 tablespooons of oil. Add rice and stir until grains are coated with oil. Combine the broth and wine and pour 2 cups of liquid over the rice. Add saffron and season with salt. When liquid is absorbed, stir in 1 cup liquid, increase heat to medium-high, and bring to a boil, stirring occasionally. When liquid is absorbed again, stir in an additional cup. Transfer rice mixture to an ovenproof serving dish with a lid. Press chicken into rice and spoon ham and chorizo over. Cover and bake until the rice is cooked and slightly creamy, 20 to 30 minutes. (You may have to add the remaining cup of liquid if the mixture gets too dry).

Turn oven off. Sprinkle peas over rice, cover, and place dish in oven until seafood is cooked.

Saute shrimp, scallops, and monkfish or cod separately until cooked through (each will take about 2 minutes to cook). Arrange seafood over rice and garnish with roasted red pepper strips. Sprinkle with parsley and serve.

Juanita's accident gets Gabrielle thinking about her own behavior and the extent to which she has put her own needs and desires before anyone else's. As she wonders whether her mother-in-law may die in part due to her own illicit affair, she comes close to confessing to a priest. When she is unable to, she decides instead to throw a charity fashion show. It is at the show that Susan discovers Gabrielle's affair and calls her on her lack of ethics. "You're beautiful, you have more money than you can spend and you have a husband that adores you," Susan tells her, and for the first time Gabrielle wonders if maybe she's right.

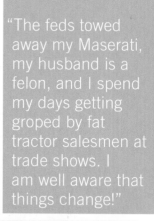

42

Feeling her conscience stirred, Gabrielle confesses to John's mother, who intimates that there will be hell to pay. When the police come to the Solises' door, a terrified Gabrielle starts to tell Carlos the truth, but it turns out to be the FBI, who arrest Carlos for unfair business practices.

When the police freeze the family's assets, this pampered trophy wife is forced to get a job. But she has faced hardship before — as a model, she pulled herself up from nothing and isn't afraid to do so again. She comforts Carlos, telling him "poor" is just a state of mind. "You're a strong woman, Gaby," he says, and he's right.

It is at the end of the season that Gabrielle begins to come into her own, maturing from a sheltered prima donna into a brave and uncompromising woman. When an unlikely benefactor, Bree, offers to lend them money, Gabrielle puts her pride aside and graciously accepts.

As it begins to look like Gabrielle and Carlos are getting on their feet again, she learns that she is pregnant — and that Carlos tampered with her birth control. Unsure who the father is, she elects to keep the baby, but tells Carlos — arrested once again because of his rage-aholism — that he will be responsible for raising it.

FOR THE SCENE WHERE GABRIELLE AND CARLOS ARE WASHING THEIR CLOTHES IN THE TUB, EVA LONGORIA WORE HER OWN BIKINI.

Dressing Gabrielle

URBAN CHIC, PROVACATIVE, FUSCHIA

When Adair shops for Gabrielle, she tends to keep in mind both Gabrielle's present life — a housewife in the suburbs — and her past life, as a hot runway model. "When I go out shopping for Gabrielle," says Adair, "I look for urban chic, because she's had that life in New York. So even if she's moved to the suburbs and she's living with Carlos, I try to come at it from that perspective."

Carlos — she is often in little more than a teddy, or a bra and panties. Her lingerie is a mix of Victoria's Secret, Elle MacPherson, Betsey Johnson, and high-end designers like La Perla and Cosabella. "She has worn lingerie from just about every designer out there. Just as we think we've found every one, there's another one that comes up that we get really excited about."

Unlike the other housewives, Gabrielle dresses up for almost every activity — even to go shopping. She likes being noticed and she likes dressing provocatively. "So her colors are often just a little bit hotter and brighter than anyone else's," says Adair. "We use a lot of pink on the show and if Gabrielle is wearing pink, it's very hot pink, or bubblegum, or extremely fuchsia."

But what tends to garner more attention than Gabrielle's clothes is her lack of them. Since she has so many sex scenes — both with John and

"I didn't realize I was going to wear so much lingerie," says Eva Longoria. "I knew Gabrielle would have an affair, but I didn't know she'd be in lingerie all the time. So I had to hire a personal trainer. But I think on the show it's merited. She's definitely using her sexuality as a tool and a weapon. And what I like about our show is the clothes are not a character as they were on *Sex and the City*. I like that they're still secondary to who we are and how we play things. So I don't really focus so much on the clothes — other than that Gabrielle is always inappropriately dressed."

What's fascinating about Gabrielle's affair, and what we've found in the writing, is that we can make her so selfish. She does these selfish, horrible things, and Eva Longoria is so beautiful and charming, it's amazing what she gets away with. If you're going to have someone doing awful things, it really helps if they're personally charming. — Marc Cherry

44

an interview with
EVA LONGORIA

IT POPPED

I thought the pilot was the most brilliant thing I had read in a long time. It literally popped. It just jumped out at me. It was funny, it was mysterious, and it left me wanting more.

I went in on the first day of casting, and I was the first actor cast. I thought, *Well, I'm not going to get this just because they probably don't even know what they want yet.* But Marc Cherry said he was really specific as to what he wanted for Gabrielle, and after they cast me he said, "You came in, and you were the first [Gabrielle audition], and then it was downhill from there."

BIRTHDAY
MARCH 15

HOMETOWN
CORPUS CHRISTI, TEXAS

Voted by *Variety* as one of the "Ten New Faces to Watch," by *USA Today* as one of "Fall TV's Hot 11" and *TV Guide* as one of their "New Faces of Fall," Longoria is a star on the rise. She recently costarred in the CBS movie-of-the-week *The Dead Will Tell,* in which she played a quirky psychic named Jenny, whose mental abilities play an intricate part in solving a murder. In the 2003–04 season she starred on *L.A. Dragnet,* Emmy Award–winning producer Dick Wolf's modern-day take on the classic police drama.

Voted one of *Maxim* magazine's "Hot 100" for 2004 (and voted #1 for 2005), one of *People en Espanol's* "25 Most Beautiful People," one of *People's* 2005 "50 Most Beautiful" and winner of an ALMA Award for "Outstanding Actress in a Daytime Drama," Eva is also known for her role as Isabella Williams on the *Young and the Restless,* a role she played for three seasons.

Eva regularly appears in *Hot Tamales Live,* a critically lauded comedy/variety show at The Comedy Store in which she both stars and co-produces. Previously she celebrated her theater debut in the popular comedy farce, *What the Rabbi Saw.* She has appeared in the films *Carlita's Secret, Harsh Times,* and *The Sentinel.*

I don't think Gabrielle comes from an evil place. I think she's just confused and she's trying to find her happiness and going about it the wrong way. It's been exciting to do these scenes in the second half of the season where she shows more depth, like the speeches she has with Carlos when they are broke. You see that vulnerable side of her and then you realize she's human. I want Gabrielle to have as many colors and as much range as possible so people like her. She's a great character, but when I started the show, I thought, *Oh my God, this is the woman that everybody's going to hate.* And everybody's really come to like her. I'm pleasantly surprised by that.

My favorite line is the one in the pilot where she says she got everything she wanted but wanted all the wrong things. That's what life's about: discovering that what you end up with is not what you thought you wanted. What we all want and need is constantly changing, so it's okay to change your mind. You don't have to live in a mistake. That's the big moral of many of the show's storylines.

I DECIDED TO STAY

I got into acting through pageants in Texas. The last pageant I won was Miss Corpus Christi USA. And in that prize package was a scholarship to come to L.A. and compete in a modeling and talent competition. I won every category I was in. I had thirty agents wanting to sign me, and I decided to stay.

THE EXACT OPPOSITE OF ME

Gabrielle is the exact opposite of me, which is always fun. She's very challenging because she doesn't have any moral boundaries. She doesn't live by any codes. She's not a good wife, she's not a mother, she's not a great neighbor, and she's pretty selfish. So as an actor it's really fun to play someone who has so many colors. I would like to think I'm more selfless than she is. And I love family. I would love to have kids.

There are a lot of women that don't want children, and the fact that society expects you to once you're married is absurd because you can have a very fulfilling life without kids. It's totally normal to be married and not have kids, and I love representing that little slice of life for whoever is out there and identifies with it.

By having her affair with John she's just trying to change something. When you do that you're definitely going to come to a crossroads. Unconsciously she's creating this drama so she has to face a decision.

A PIECE OF ALL OF US

The Solises are very pioneering in the way that the Cosbys were. They were a lawyer and a doctor who were African-American and well-off. That was never heard of on TV. I think it's the same thing for the Solises. We're the richest couple on the block and we have a white gardener, which is unheard of in our society. It's a great thing to see Latinos portrayed in a positive way. I'm a huge activist for Latino rights and it's a fact that Latinos are still severely underrepresented in television and in film, so any time any Latino is cast, I think that it's great.

Erotic

EDIE BRITT

**A TALL
DRINK
OF WATER**

Edie Britt is the most reviled woman on Wisteria Lane, and yet her charm is that she doesn't really understand why. Strong-willed and self-employed, when Edie sees something she wants, she goes after it. And nothing will stand in her way. Twice divorced, a knockout, and a legendary loose woman, when Edie learns that a handsome eligible bachelor has moved onto the block she sets out to get him, even though Susan has gotten there first. Edie will do anything to land Mike — cozy up to his dog, bring over ambrosia or sausage puttanesca, hire him to do plumbing work, even ride a mechanical bull so he can see.

It's no wonder Edie is the way she is — she is a self-made realtor and single mother who came from the wrong side of the tracks and had a troubled childhood. So at an early age, she learned not to rely on anyone but herself. But she is misunderstood by the women of Wisteria Lane, who view her as a menace and a threat. If any character highlights the cliquishness and snobbery of suburban women, it is Edie, who is shunned by nearly every woman in the neighborhood.

Edie's only friend is the neighborhood gossip, Mrs. Huber, an outcast in her own right; and when Mrs. Huber is murdered, Edie is truly bereft. Edie asks the housewives to scatter Martha's ashes with her, but none of them are willing to make the trip except Susan, who complies for selfish reasons.

On their rowboat ride, Susan confesses that she burned Edie's house down and Edie is furious. When Susan begs forgiveness, Edie uses it as an

"Your foreman said that you were on a date with a hottie. Evidently someone's in need of LASIK."

47

opportunity to get something she wants: acceptance from the women of the neighborhood. She wrangles her way into their weekly poker game, determined to have entry even if she will never truly be liked. But Edie wants to learn the way camaraderie works, seeking advice from Lynette about how she can be a good friend. When she finds that Susan is suffering over her breakup with Mike, Edie shows surprising kindness — taking Susan out for a rollicking night on the town.

"Of course I believe in evil.
I work in real estate."

48

1 CAN (20 OZ)
Pineapple chunks, drained

1 CAN (11 OZ)
Mandarin oranges, drained

1 CUP
Chopped walnuts

1 CUP
Sour cream

1 BAG (10.5 OZ)
Miniature marshmallows

1 CUP
Maraschino cherries

IN A LARGE BOWL, COMBINE ALL INGREDIENTS EXCEPT MARSHMALLOWS AND CHERRIES. REFRIGERATE FOR AT LEAST 1 HOUR AND UP TO 2 DAYS. JUST BEFORE SERVING, ADD MARSHMALLOWS AND CHERRIES AND TOSS TO COMBINE. SERVE CHILLED OR AT ROOM TEMPERATURE.

The women wind up breaking into Paul Young's house to get to the bottom of Mrs. Huber's murder, and Paul unexpectedly comes home early. So Edie once again looks to her biggest assets for help, seducing Paul so that Susan can sneak out of the house. But her friendship with Susan is short-lived, and before she knows it, she is warring with Susan again — over a contractor, then over Mike again after Susan and Mike get back together. And when Susan, with a gun in her back, really needs Edie's help, Edie misunderstands and calls Susan a bitch. It seems these two will fight until the bitter end.

Dressing Edie

SHORT SHORTS, PROVOCATIVE, EXTREME

"Edie dresses for the occasion," says Adair, and truer words were never spoken. "Edie's character will say, 'I'm gonna wash my car and I'm gonna make sure that everybody watches me washing my car, so what's a great outfit to get wet in?' Or she'll say, 'I'm going to go and sell a house. And I still need to feel body-conscious. I have to wear a blazer, but how many buttons do I have undone, shorts she wore while washing her car. Sheridan went out and bought that outfit herself. "They wanted something sexy, but I wanted something sexy that looked normal. So it was just a pair of Abercrombie & Fitch shorts and a little cheap white cotton shirt, but there was an expensive bra made by Agent Provocateur underneath."

and how short is the skirt, and how do I walk in it?' She's driven by the occasion and who's watching her on that particular occasion."

Of course, we have rarely seen Edie covered up—nearly every outfit she wears shows off her ample bosom and never-ending legs. As Nicollette Sheridan puts it, "Edie always dresses to get male attention. I think it makes her feel good about herself. I'm the opposite."

Adair's favorite items are the little black funeral dress that Edie wears when she buries Mrs. Huber's ashes, and the now-notorious short

The extreme costumes help Sheridan inhabit her role and find the visual comedy in her work. "There's a bit of physical comedy in that scene where I was washing the car. I was scrubbing one way with my hand and swinging my butt the other way."

Though it's easy to make jokes about Edie's revealing costumes, Sheridan points out that there is one outfit Edie has never worn on the show: lingerie. "Edie's never even been seen in her underwear. She's never even had a love scene in the show. All the other trollops have, but she hasn't."

an interview with
NICOLLETTE SHERIDAN

Nicollette Sheridan, born in England and raised in London and Los Angeles, is best known to TV audiences for her role as the beautiful, powerful, and manipulative Paige Matheson in the long-running drama series, *Knots Landing.* Her other television credits include TV miniseries and movies such as *Lucky Chances, Indictment: The McMartin Trial, The People Next Door, The Spiral Staircase,* and *Dead Husbands.* She also appeared in the TV movie thriller *Transplant* directed by Michael Scott and produced by Harvey Kahn.

Sheridan has appeared in many feature films. Her first was in the hit Rob Reiner comedy *The Sure Thing,* in which she played the object of John Cusack's cross-country quest to find "the sure thing." She has also starred in the comedies *Noises Off* with Michael Caine and Carol Burnett, *Spy Hard* opposite Leslie Nielsen, and *Beverly Hills Ninja* with Chris Farley and Chris Rock. Sheridan is also the spokesperson for NuGlow.

I never saw Edie as a big part of the show. I thought Edie was going to be just this tiny little recurring part. And when Nicollette Sheridan, an established TV presence, agreed to be a part of the show, the role got much, much bigger. That was a lucky thing to happen. There's a saying that my friends in the business have, 'Sometimes the casting gods are with you, and sometimes they're not.' And in this one the casting gods were showering their blessings on us. — Marc Cherry

THAT WAS IT

I was born in England but we moved here when I was ten, and in my senior year my mother ended up sending me back to England. It was a very artsy school, and I was asked to help codirect this play. So I agreed to do that and then the next thing I knew I was in it. I had never had the acting bug. I got my first line out and that was it. I've been acting ever since.

I moved back to the States and signed with Elite Models and a commercial agent who is still my agent and dear friend. She sent me out on twelve auditions for commercials, and I got each and every one of them. I was a Flex girl, I did No-Nonsense Pantyhose, milk, body spray, Jell-O, and A1 Steak Sauce. As I was doing the commercials I thought, *God, I really wish I had more to say* and *This is really fun. It speaks to me.* So I did the pilot for *Paper Dolls* and the movie *The Sure Thing.*

I really took to Edie because she's a lot of fun to play. She is just a very strong, forthright force to be reckoned with. She goes after what she wants in such a way that the women on Wisteria Lane feel threatened by her. She is an outsider, and I think people identify with that because at some point in one's life you've felt like you didn't fit into a certain group or situation.

People always say, "Oh, gosh, I love Edie and she's so mean." I don't see her as being mean. I see her as someone who goes after what she wants, and she puts herself first, which is something I need to learn to do a little bit more in my life. She's just brutally forthright. She's not a bad person. She's not cheating on anyone. She hasn't killed anyone. She's not a liar.

FORTY IS TODAY'S THIRTY

We all do a lot of laughing while we're working and it's wonderful. Now people are writing pilots about fortysomething women. We have pioneered the way. Forty is today's thirty.

Sometimes it's hard for me when Edie has to be mean to Susan because I like Teri so much. At the end of the scene it's like, "Come here and let me give you a hug." She's a good sport about it, and we just have this amazing chemistry together.

IT WASN'T A WHOLEHEARTED COMMITMENT

I read the pilot for *Desperate Housewives* and loved it. It was wickedly funny, very human, different, and most of all, extremely entertaining. They wanted me to come in and read for Bree, who I thought was a very interesting, complicated, uptight nightmare. I thought, *If this show goes for seven years I would want to pull my hair out playing this role. But if this is the only one they really see me as, then all right. I'll go in and read for it.*

So I went in and was committed to the reading, but it wasn't a wholehearted commitment because the suit that I wore really wasn't something that Bree would wear. It was a beautiful white Chloé pantsuit with a plunging neckline. So I read for Bree and at the end the director looked at me and he said, "No, no, no." I said, "Excuse me? 'No, no, no'? What the hell is that supposed to mean?" And he said, "I see you as Edie. Would you mind playing a character like that?" So I went out, unbuttoned a couple of buttons of my jacket, brushed my hair, came back in and read for Edie. They laughed out loud. It was pretty much a done deal. I said, "I come in a good wife, mother of two, and I leave the slut. It's a shoo-in."

"MARTHA HUBER WAITED HER WHOLE LIFE FOR SOMETHING TO HAPPEN TO HER. BUT THE YEARS HAD GONE BY AND STILL NOTHING EXCITING HAD EVER HAPPENED TO MARTHA HUBER. UNTIL THE NIGHT SHE WAS MURDERED."

Malicious MARTHA HUBER

THE NOSY NEIGHBOR

Mrs. Huber's HARANGUES

MRS. HUBER
I was just thinking of that expression, "I'll make mincemeat out of you." Mincemeat used to be an entrée made up of mostly chopped meat. So it was like saying, "I'll chop you up into little bits."

MRS. HUBER
Being coy is a strategy best employed by virgins at their first dance. For women of our age, it's just annoying.

MRS. HUBER
If you're missing money, I'd ask one of those strange men you parade through here at all hours.

EDIE
I am not going to apologize for having a healthy sex life.

MRS. HUBER
Healthy? I'm going to have to burn every sheet you've touched.

MRS. HUBER
My idiot husband died and left me with a worthless pension. I was desperate for money. And it's better to take it from a bad person than a good one. How was I supposed to know she'd shoot herself?

PAUL
She was a good person.

MRS. HUBER
A good person who leaves her child motherless? Read the Bible, Paul. Suicide's a big no-no.

Fans were devastated to see Martha Huber go — if only because she was so much fun to watch. Mrs. Huber said the things everyone was thinking (but no one wanted to say) and she did it with a smile, pleasantly diabolical.

It wasn't too surprising that Mrs. Huber was Mary Alice's blackmailer, since she had already tried to blackmail Susan. Mrs. Huber never viewed her actions as anything less than necessary, putting her own needs before the pain and anguish she might cause others.

Mrs. Huber's most infuriating quality was her honesty — honesty to the point of recklessness. She mocked Edie's loose ways, told Lynette how to raise her children, and made the fatal mistake of telling Paul Young why Mary Alice deserved to die. When he hit her with the blender and then choked her to death, it begged the question just who on Wisteria Lane was going to tell the God's honest truth.

an interview with
CHRISTINE ESTABROOK

Marc Cherry ran into me at a deli in L.A. in 2002, and he said, "I'm writing a part for you." Two years later he calls me on the phone and he says, "Listen. I've finished this pilot. It's Mrs. Huber and I want you to come in and read for it." A month goes by and I don't hear from him and then it comes out in the breakdown that they're going to make the woman Asian. Her name has been changed to Mrs. Chang. So I called him and he said the network wanted the cast more ethnically diverse. Another month goes by and he calls me and says, "Can you come in and audition tomorrow?" So I went in and read for Mrs. Chang and I got it.

I really liked this character. I thought she had quite an interesting set of ethics. I think that she feels when there's wrongdoing, like with Susan not coming forward about her setting fire to Edie's home, that it's fair game. It's better to blackmail someone who is nasty or who's done something wrong than someone who's a good person.

BIRTHDAY
SEPTEMBER 13

HOMETOWN
EAST AURORA, NEW YORK

After graduating from the prestigious Yale School of Drama, Estabrook quickly made her mark in the theater, starring in Broadway productions of *The Sisters Rosenzweig, The Heidi Chronicles, I'm Not Rappaport, The Inspector General,* and *The Cherry Orchard.* She won a Drama Desk Award for the Off-Broadway production of *The Boys Next Door,* an Obie award for her role in *Pastorale,* and a Drama Desk Award nomination for her performance in *North Shore Fish.* Estabrook's credits also include numerous regional theater productions, and four years working in the Eugene O'Neill Playwrights Conference.

After 17 years of performing on stage, Estabrook decided she was ready for new challenges and moved to Los Angeles, eager to work in a different medium. Since then, she has guest starred on some of television's most popular shows, such as *Frasier, Dharma & Greg, Touched by an Angel, 7th Heaven, Chicago Hope, Crossing Jordan,* and *Six Feet Under.* Her film work includes *Sea of Love, Presumed Innocent, The Usual Suspects,* and *Spiderman 2.*

53

Desperate HUSBANDS

It's impossible to grasp just how powerful love is.
It can sustain us through trying times or motivate us to make
extraordinary sacrifices. It can force decent
men to commit the darkest deeds or compel ordinary women
to search for hidden truths. And long after
we're gone, love remains, burned into our memories.

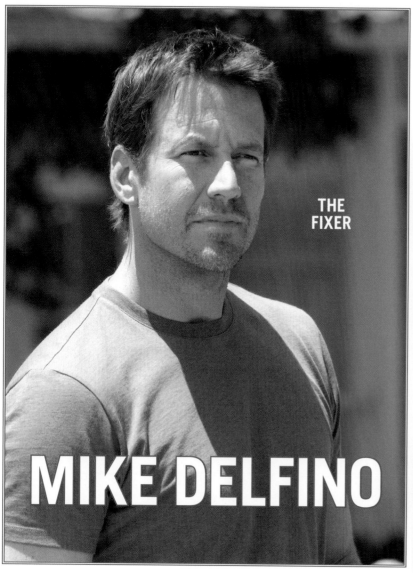

THE FIXER

MIKE DELFINO

"I always saw the character of Mike Delfino as the sex symbol for women in their mid- to late-30s," says Cherry. "He's a guy who's nice, not too pretty but certainly earthy and attractive, who can fix things." In keeping with his idea that Mike was a "fixer," Cherry decided to make him a plumber.

"Mike's a good guy," says Cherry. "The fact that he's secretive is the only flaw he has, because he's such a tremendous human being. We needed to give him a couple of flaws to make it interesting. His secrets became the character flaws."

Susan and Mike seem made for each other. Both single and middle-aged, they know what it's like to have loved and lost, which is what first connects them in the vet's office, when Susan realizes it might take some time for Mike to get over his wife. "When people meet later in life," says Cherry, "they're going to have some history. That's what makes dating so hard. You have to decide how much of someone's past you're willing to deal with."

Thwarted again and again by Edie (or Mrs. Huber's blackmailing), they keep coming back to each other. It's a case of opposites attracting. He's serious; she's kooky. He's secretive; she's ridiculously up front. And yet (and this is why we like him so much), Mike was the one who said, "I love you" first, and kissed Susan first, and who keeps coming back after he's arrested to try to explain to her just who he is. And after their end-of-season reunion, Mike may not only save Susan's heart, but her life.

an interview with
JAMES DENTON

Right away I knew the show was unique in its perspective, having a real feminine voice and female characters in their thirties and forties who were real people having normal conversations. On TV, women over 40 are usually lawyers, cops, doctors, or the grieving mother of a lost child. The women on our show aren't typical but they are American women who are talking about their real lives, their exes, their husbands, their kids, and their jobs. I found that refreshing.

BIRTHDAY
JANUARY 20

HOMETOWN
NASHVILLE, TENNESSEE

Denton has appeared in such films as *Primary Colors, Face/Off,* and *That Old Feeling.* In 1997 he landed the role of the eerily sociopathic Mr. Lyle on NBC's hit drama show *The Pretender,* which was followed by *The Pretender* television films *Pretender 2001* and *Pretender: The Island of the Haunted.*

In 2001, Denton was cast by ABC to star opposite Kim Delaney in Steven Bochco's *Philly,* and his growing reputation quickly led to a role as Special Agent Jon Kilmer on *Threat Matrix.* In addition to his series roles on television, his guest appearances include *J.A.G., Sliders, Dark Skies, Two Guys and a Girl, Ally McBeal,* and *The West Wing.*

Mike is a guy with a truck and a dog, so that tells you something. My wife said when she met me and saw that I had a dog and a pickup truck, she knew she was dead.

57

Mike and I are similar in that he's letting his romantic side get in the way of his goals. He's in the neighborhood for a specific purpose, and he doesn't need to be getting tied up with Susan. I've led my whole life letting women become a distraction. There's a single-mindedness to him that I relate to, a goal-oriented nature. But he's very secretive and I'm not. He's got a real checkered past and he's been in trouble with the law. He's a hell of a lot more interesting than I am.

The show is successful because they did everything right. If you cast any other women in Hollywood, this show might not work. They're all so different and so perfect for their roles. And the male characters are fleshed out a lot more deeply than anyone thought they were going to be. People thought it would just be a chick show and the guys would be props.

Every interview I do, people want to know about how the women get along, about catfights and competition. I think it's sexist to assume that they don't get along. I've been on shows with a whole bunch of men, and nobody ever asked me that.

There's a real maturity on this set. We're not a bunch of kids. Almost all of us are parents, so our set is a lot more family-like and a lot less Hollywood. People are talking to their kids on their phones instead of their agents, talking about daycare as opposed to what films they're trying to do on hiatus.

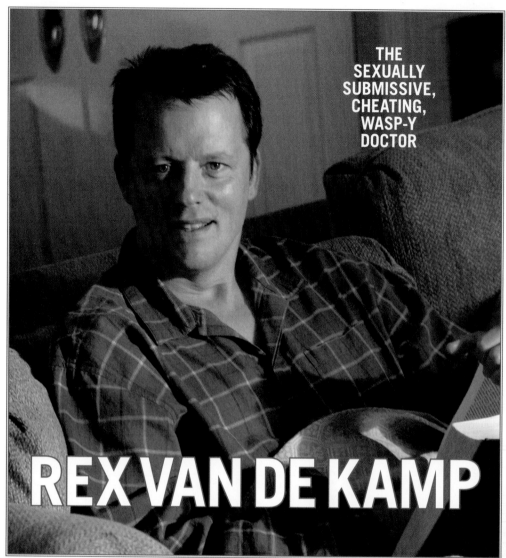

THE SEXUALLY SUBMISSIVE, CHEATING, WASP-Y DOCTOR

REX VAN DE KAMP

Rex Van de Kamp has surprised us more than any other man on Wisteria Lane. The staid, WASPy doctor has turned out to be a submissive john with a penchant for being handcuffed to the bed.

Complex and troubled, Rex was nonetheless in love with Bree, even though he couldn't admit it sometimes. At first it seemed all of their marital problems were Bree's fault, but quickly it became clear that Rex was the truly elusive partner. Rex was the one who couldn't open up fully, sexually, because he was afraid to tell Bree just what he liked. Her openness and persistence forced him to admit to his preferences — and when he did he seemed like a liberated man.

Over the first season, Rex and Bree had ups and downs, but each time Bree pulled away, Rex reeled her in, and vice versa. Though Rex tried to buy his children's affection, solicited prostitution, hid his sexual fetish, and meddled in Bree's dating life, he always seemed oddly right for Bree. This is what made their strange love affair so captivating.

"I feel bad for him," says Cherry, "because he has done so many horrible things to Bree. He is so reviled across the country. But Steven Culp, fortunately, has had a really good time doing it, and I've always been very appreciative of that."

When Bree lost him at the end of Season One, the audience couldn't help but feel sad for her. A new chapter of her life was about to begin, but she had lost her first and only love. She might find other men, but she will never find another Rex.

You hate to tell an actor as he's signing on, "By the way, you're going to be dead by the end of the year."
— MARC CHERRY

BIRTHDAY

DECEMBER 3

HOMETOWN

LA JOLLA, CALIFORNIA

Even before his critically acclaimed performance as Robert F. Kennedy in the theatrical film *Thirteen Days* brought him to the attention of moviegoers, Steven Culp had already attracted a large following among television fans for his recurring role as the mysterious CIA agent Clayton Webb on the CBS series *J.A.G.* In the 2003–2004 season he also appeared on *The West Wing, E.R.,* and *Star Trek: Enterprise.*

Culp's films include *The Emperor's Club, Spartan, Nurse Betty, James and the Giant Peach, Fearless,* and *Dead Again.*

an interview with
STEVEN CULP

The show works because it's really entertaining. Beyond that, I think that there are things that resonate in people's lives. Rex and Bree's relationship is about, *How do you keep passion alive over a long marriage? How do you keep love alive?* As far out as we get, there's truth in a lot of what we do.

That's true of Rex's little peccadillo—you go on the Internet to chat rooms and you realize there are a lot of people out there who are like Rex, who have fantasies or things that they're afraid to tell their partner.

From the beginning, Rex's character has been confused. All he knows is he doesn't want to be where he is. He doesn't know where he wants to go and wouldn't know how to get there if he did. He's got these secrets that he's compartmentalized or denied and now he's finally acting on them. The more the character has unraveled, the more I've been digging it.

Marc and I had discussed early on, "What is Rex thinking about when he's by himself?" About five episodes in, he gave me this assignment to see if I could find a fetish. So I was Googling around, looking at sexual fetishes and I came up with the idea that he was into drag kings, women dressed as men. But Marc finally decided on S&M, and I think it turned out to be the best decision.

At the beginning you thought Rex and Bree were just one thing, but their relationship has taken on the levels of a real couple that's been married for eighteen years. In some ways, they're really made for each other, but through the pressures of marriage and kids, they became distant.

Sometimes I joke that we could be doing exactly what we're doing, but if you called the show *Desperate Husbands,* people might be a little more sympathetic to Rex. But that's just part of the package.

What I like about Rex and Bree is that we're able to go from the episode where she gets the secret out of him, to watching the tape, to trying to do it and pick a safe word. We go from really intense dramatic moments to high comedy and back again. It's really exhilarating.

59

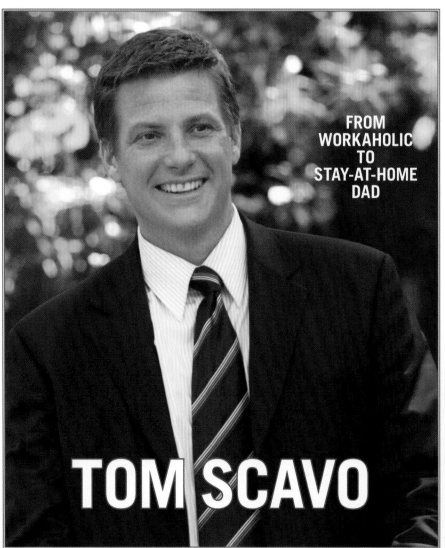

FROM WORKAHOLIC TO STAY-AT-HOME DAD

TOM SCAVO

60

The character of Tom is based on Marc Cherry's father, who traveled frequently when Cherry was a child. "He would go away for business trips for six months at a time," Cherry remembers. "When he wasn't there it would just be my mom with us kids."

Tom is often oblivious to how difficult Lynette's life is. He can't open a Jell-O container, but refuses to admit he's inept at taking care of the kids. Tom's most winning quality is that he adores Lynette even when she drives him crazy, and he seldom says, "I told you so," even when he can. He knows deep down that Lynette holds the cards in the relationship, and that he'd be devastated if he lost her. The most surprising change to their relationship is at the end of Season One when Tom quits his job and tells Lynette to go back to work.

"So often it's just assumed the man will be the breadwinner, and the woman will stay home," says Cherry. "This country is filled with brilliant women who probably should be the breadwinner and men who should take over the housekeeping duties. But that's just not the way society looks at it."

I gave Doug my word of honor that he would be a regular in Season Two, so he signed up. I'm so glad we did it because he's turned out to be one of my favorite people on the show and he's had tremendous chemistry with Felicity. — MARC CHERRY

BIRTHDAY

JUNE 21

HOMETOWN

LOS ANGELES, CALIFORNIA

Doug Savant began his acting career when he left UCLA to perform in Los Angeles regional theater. He went on to appear in such films as *Masquerade, Hanoi Hilton, Godzilla,* and *Red Surf.*

While Savant is perhaps most recognizable from his role of Matt Fielding on Fox's *Melrose Place,* he has starred in many television films, including the TBS thriller trilogy: *First Show, First Target,* and *First Daughter.* He had a recurring role on the hit Fox series *24* and has made memorable guest appearances on several series, including *N.Y.P.D. Blue, J.A.G.,* and *Nip/Tuck.* His theater work includes *Relay, You Never Can Tell,* and *When the Jacaranda Blooms.*

Women approach me a lot and say, "You are my husband. He travels all the time and he comes home and he just expects so much of me."

We did some international press coverage and I found that this show is the highest rated in the history of all of television in Australia. The Channel Four people in Great Britain said, "We carried the premieres of all the hit American television shows—*Sex and the City, Friends*—and the premiere of *Desperate Housewives* outnumbered them all."

It made me feel good that somehow our lives may be similar to those of people in all these foreign countries. They behave the same as we do and worry about the same subjects. Somewhere in Bulgaria there's a Wisteria Lane.

Tom and I are similar in that we are passionately in love with our wives and love our kids. I have four children too. But there are times when Tom is inattentive to what's going on. The way I see it, Tom's not a bad husband in the least. He thinks he's a good husband. He's just oblivious to what Lynette's problems could be.

When we were shooting the scenes where Lynette and I are fighting about Annabel, it was hard for me. Every time I have conflict with Lynette on the show, it doesn't make me feel real good. Sins of omission are okay. Sins of commission are more problematic because they spell real trouble.

The thing I like about Lynette and Tom's relationship on the show is that these people love each other. I think we're the couple that most reflects the problems that real people have, in that we are trying to balance work and the personal needs of two adults while trying to raise this large family. That's what most people can relate to.

CARLOS
If you talk to Al Mason at this thing I want you to casually mention how much I paid for your necklace.

GABRIELLE
Why don't I just pin the receipt to my chest?

CARLOS
He let me know how much he paid for his wife's new convertible. Look, just work it into the conversation.

GABRIELLE
There's no way I can just work that in, Carlos.

CARLOS
Why not? At the Donahue party, everyone was talking mutual funds. And you found a way to mention you slept with half the Yankee outfield.

GABRIELLE
Every time I'm around that man he tries to grab my ass!

CARLOS
I made over two hundred thousand doing business with him last year. If he wants to grab your ass, let him.

CARLOS
Now who the hell is that? And look at how she's touching him. You think that's the guy she's having the affair with?

JUANITA
Carlos, don't be stupid. A guy she talks to in public isn't someone you're gonna worry about.

CARLOS
So it's someone that she doesn't talk to? What do I have to do, beat up every guy in town?

AN
ALPHA MALE
ON HIS
WAY DOWN
THE
LADDER

CARLOS SOLIS

Ricardo was it. He was the only one we saw who had the necessary looks and gravitas to pull it off.
— MARC CHERRY

Powerful, angry, and temperamental, Carlos Solis is the kind of man you'd be terrified to see your daughter marry. Yet Carlos has a soft side too. He seldom puts his feelings into words, but he shows Gabrielle his love by buying her things, like a bracelet or a Maserati, and believes these gestures are meaningful. He is slowly realizing that Gabrielle does not love him, and at the end of Season One, he learns that she has had an affair with John, their teenaged gardener.

As their relationship evolved over the course of the first season, both Gabrielle and Carlos showed they were forces to be reckoned with. Their temporary emotional reunion was followed by a scary and violent fight.

"The violence is connected to this very fiery, spicy relationship," says Cherry, "where the passion can go the wrong way or the right way, depending upon the mood." It is unclear how these two mercurial souls will find a way to raise a child.

an interview with
RICARDO ANTONIO CHAVIRA

One of the reasons the show is so popular is because people would always rather laugh and talk about someone else's dirty laundry than their own. People are gossips, *chismosas,* as we say in Spanish. Mrs. Huber is la chismosa. On Monday mornings at work people talk about the show and it sparks communication between the sexes. It makes for a better relationship. Maybe the guy really wants to have a baby and the woman's not so sure. And then that birth control scene pops up. What kind of conversation happens on that couch? I bet women who saw that picked a whole new place to keep their birth control.

This show is perfect for our times because of all the problems that we have been facing: the socioeconomic issues in our country. There's not a lot of happiness going on out there in the world. People are struggling. Gas prices are high. Jobs are getting cut. You need something to distract yourself. When you watch Gabrielle and Carlos doing their laundry in the hot tub, you can at least laugh about it. It distracts you just enough to make things bearable.

There was so much that appealed to me about the pilot. Number one, you've got Latinos and they're the richest family on the block. But they don't beat you over the head with the fact that the Solises are Latino. They could have been any race.

The other thing that I found great with respect to my character was that, here's this guy who's very powerful, very rich, and very Latino. He's obviously got a macho streak to him. But he's a cuckold. Normally, the Latino guy is the Don Juan. He'd be the one having the affair. So I thought it was really interesting.

I had a darker, more macho side when I was younger. From ages 18 to 21 that was pretty much the face that I wore whenever I interacted with the world. Now that I'm older I don't do that. Especially with the birth of my son, I try to make things work out. But I can tap into that other side when I need to and it is pretty scary, even for myself. That side is very much my father. He's a judge. He's very nice. He's very judicious. But if you corner him and you put him on the spot, he's going to let you know to back up. I can do that too, without having to do anything physically, just with words and with my intention.

63

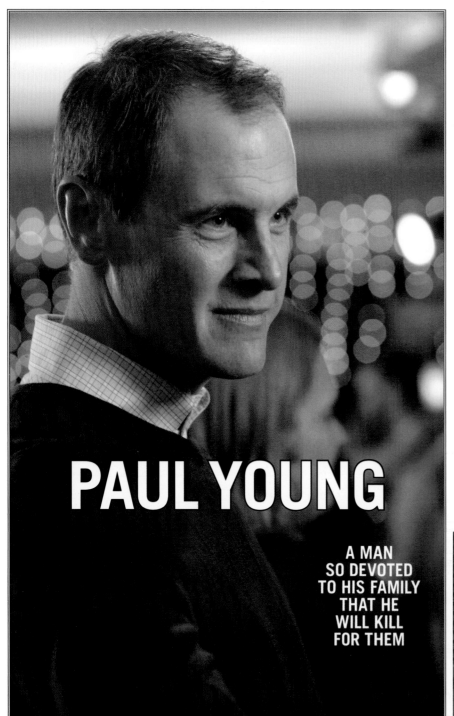

PAUL YOUNG

**A MAN
SO DEVOTED
TO HIS FAMILY
THAT HE
WILL KILL
FOR THEM**

If Paul Young is ever arrested for his two crimes, you could imagine neighbors telling the news reporters "He was always sort of a weirdo." Pleasant-looking enough, he exudes an eerie quality that makes his neighbors uncomfortable. And rightly so. This is a man who buried a dead body in his pool and murdered Mrs. Huber with his bare hands.

And yet what keeps Paul from being completely unsympathetic is his passionate love for Mary Alice. He laments his wife's death and can't get over it.

Though there were several times over the course of the first season when we wondered whether the Youngs might move, we always wanted them to stay. Every neighborhood, like every family, needs someone to gossip about. For Paul Young, life is not a joking matter and one's neighbors have no right to pry into one's personal business. If anyone tries to tell him otherwise, well, she'd better watch out … or she might end up like Martha Huber.

At the end of Season One Paul got his comeuppance as his son was taken away and he was almost killed by Mike Delfino. But as he explained what happened, Mike took pity on him and left him alone in the desert to disappear forever … or maybe, just maybe, to return to Wisteria Lane.

Mark is such a nice guy. I didn't really think he would have the gravitas to pull off the underlying insidiousness of Paul Young. But time has given him some insight into the dark side of people. — MARC CHERRY

an interview with

MARK MOSES

I was on a panel and someone asked, "How do you sleep at night?" I said, "I sleep fine. I'm not sure Paul Young sleeps well. I have a feeling he tosses and turns a lot." The great thing about being an actor is that you put yourself in situations that you hope you'd never encounter in real life, but you can use your imagination and go there.

I've done a lot of roles that have been comedic or friendly dads or nice guys and this was a nice turn. I can relate to a lot of Paul's issues. I understand his drive to keep his family as a unit. Every family has skeletons in the closet. I grew up in Evansville, Illinois, and my street was like *Peyton Place.* Wives left for other people on the block, and sometimes there were divorces. People did talk and there was gossip, like on Wisteria Lane.

On a lot of shows, as in Hollywood in general, there aren't a lot of great roles for women who are forty or over. This is great in that respect. On other shows it becomes a very guy-oriented set. There's less time in hair and makeup. When I did *Platoon* years ago, it was a little water and dirt in your face and you were off. It was two seconds. Here, hair and makeup is a big deal in that it takes more time.

But on the other hand it's a great thing because there should be more opportunities for women to work when they get older. These are the best roles that are available in the business right now for women over forty.

Men and women both say to me, "I didn't really want to really watch it. I thought it was a soap opera thing. And then I watched it. Damn it, Mark, I'm hooked!" You know the show's a hit when you go to the grocery store and people say, "Hey, where's my *Desperate Housewives?* Where's my fix?" It's because it's good writing and the actors are well-suited to the roles and it's produced well.

BIRTHDAY
....
FEBRUARY 24

HOMETOWN
NEW YORK, NEW YORK

Mark Moses' list of television credits includes roles on NBC's *The Single Guy, In My Life, Ally McBeal* and *Grand.* He has had lead roles in such celebrated movies for television as *Saving Jessica Lynch, The James Dean Story, The Rough Riders,* and *The Tracker.*

He has guest starred on *NYPD Blue, The West Wing, Las Vegas, The District, Malcolm in the Middle, American Dreams,* and *Oliver Beene.*

Moses' impressive career includes the distinction of having worked with Oliver Stone three times: in *Platoon, Born on the Fourth of July,* and *The Doors.*

THE
GARDENER
WHO BRINGS
FLOWERS
INTO BLOOM

JOHN ROWLAND

JOHN'S JARGON

JOHN
I got something for you.
I was going to give
it to you next time
I mowed your lawn,
but since you're here—

GABRIELLE
Oh, it's a rose!

JOHN
It's not just any rose.
Look at all the petals.
There's no flaws.
It's perfect.

GABRIELLE
Oh, John.

JOHN
Just like you.

GABRIELLE
What opportunity is more
important than college?

JOHN
For the longest time,
the only thing I had
to offer you was my
heart. Mr. Solis gave
you security and I
couldn't compete.
But now he can't even
offer you that. And I can.
My business is taking
off. I can take care
of you. We can finally
be together.
*Mrs. Solis, will
you marry me?*

GABRIELLE
I have a problem with
you seeing other girls.

JOHN
Well, I have a problem
with you having a
husband. I guess we both
have to learn to deal.

The first thing to notice about teenaged gardener John Rowland were his pectoral muscles, but over the course of Season One he has revealed himself to be deeper than that: a surprisingly romantic foil to the emotionally detached Gabrielle. This idealistic young man picks her a perfect rose, tells her he loves her, even buys her an engagement ring and asks her to mary him. His affection and openness make Gabrielle all the more aware of what is missing in her marriage.

Despite her occasionally callous nature, her adultery, and her materialism, John sees something in Gabrielle that is beautiful and worthy of love. It is this love that keeps him chasing her, even after his parents try to break them apart.

John doesn't believe his feelings are youthful obsession; he thinks he sees into her soul. It is John's inner sweetness, his purity of heart, as much as those muscles that keep us eagerly awaiting his scenes. With Gabrielle pregnant and Carlos in jail, the young lovers will undoubtedly have much more to say to each other.

The character of John
as embodied by Jesse,
was my one nod
to typical soap opera
convention:
a complete hunk.
— MARC CHERRY

an interview with
JESSE METCALFE

BIRTHDAY

DECEMBER 9

HOMETOWN

WATERFORD, CONNECTICUT

After they shot the pilot they decided that they wanted to replace the gardener, get someone a little bit older. Marc had originally wanted a light, light-haired, light-skinned guy for the part, for contrast between John and Gabrielle. But I think I won them over during the audition process.

When I went overseas to the UK to do press there, they ran a story that I had to strip naked for the audition. It was totally false. I didn't even have to take my shirt off.

Jesse Metcalfe studied at the famed Tisch School of the Arts and has modeled in both the United States and Europe, a stint that ended when he joined NBC's hit soap opera *Passions*. For four years Metcalfe honed his craft while mesmerizing the daytime audience, breaking more than a few hearts with his 2004 departure from the show. His other noted performances include a guest-starring role on the WB's *Smallville* and a small role in the critically acclaimed TV movie *44 Minutes: The North Hollywood Shoot-out*.

Metcalfe is a huge sports fan and a regular on the Hollywood Knights celebrity basketball team. Off the court, he enjoys most other team sports as well as individual pursuits like snowboarding. A music lover, he is an accomplished guitarist. He's also into classic cars, especially his fully restored '67 Camaro and the more-than-occasional poker game.

67

Shooting sex scenes isn't that sexy. When there are thirty people on set watching you and you're wearing a flesh-colored Speedo, or a sock. But Eva and I get along so well that it's not that tough. And I was on a soap opera for five years, where sex scenes are par for the course. So it's not as glamorous as people think it is.

When I was eighteen I was definitely not nearly as naïve as John appears to be. He's a small town guy. I was in a serious relationship when I was sixteen, so I know what it's like to have a first love, with those feelings of excitement and nervousness and trepidation. It's easy for me to go back and draw on that. But you can't help but become a little jaded as you grow older.

This experience has changed my life completely. I went from being a somewhat known young actor to being a celebrity. The craziest thing is that a lot of older women come up to me. They ask me to take a picture with them or tell me that they have a hedge that needs trimming. And they pass me their phone numbers. It's surprising when a teenage girl comes up to you, but it's really surprising when you look over and her mom wants to take a picture too.

THE KIDS
of Wisteria Lane

When
they come,
children
change
everything.
Especially
when
they're not
invited.

Jocular
JULIE MAYER

70

Julie Mayer is her mother's daughter in more ways than one. Both Susan and Julie are extremely compassionate, often putting other people's needs before their own. They have a tendency to fall for troubled men and a hard time unraveling themselves from destructive relationships. But if anyone is the more levelheaded of the two it is Julie, who tends to mother her own mother. Like many kids of single moms, Julie often feels more like Susan's friend than her daughter, which creates problems when Susan feels the need to assert who's in charge. When Susan and Karl got divorced, Julie found herself playing shrink, best friend, and scheduler all at once — even arranging her own doctor's appointments. So when Susan becomes angry about Julie's relationship with Zach, Julie challenges her for suddenly trying to "play the mom card."

"You know, I always assumed I'd have sex for the first time before you had it again."

The relationship between Julie and Susan is one of the most convincing and relatable on the show. Julie is a precocious teenager who teases her mom about never getting any sex and who recalls the night when Susan and Mike first "did it," because Susan made heart-shaped pancakes the next morning. Julie is bright and self-sufficient and extremely mature for her age, but there are times we can see that she is really just a kid, a kid who's struggling with her parents' divorce, her emotionally needy mother, and her own adolescence. Wherever she goes in life, Julie is sure to develop into a smart, caring, and incredibly independent woman, not too different from Susan herself.

Andrea Bowen began her life as a professional performer on Broadway at the age of six, playing Young Cosette in *Les Miserables*, becoming the youngest Cosette in the show's 16-year run. She went on to originate the role of Marta Von Trapp in the Broadway revival of *The Sound of Music*, and the role of Adele in the Broadway musical production of *Jane Eyre*.

Her television work includes *Law & Order*, *Third Watch*, *That Was Then*, *Boston Public*, *Strong Medicine*, *One Tree Hill*, *Arli$$*, and *Nip/Tuck*. She has also found success as a voiceover artist, lending her vocal talents to the film *Ice Age* and two animated pilots for the Cartoon Network, *Party Wagon* and *Ben-10*.

In addition to acting, she is also an accomplished singer and dancer who enjoys swimming, horseback riding, and reading.

an interview with
ANDREA BOWEN

My dad read the pilot script first, and I remember him telling me, "It's the best script that I've read in years," and then I read it and it was just hilarious. It was so funny and so different from what they had on TV at the time. Then I got sides for Julie and I thought, *Oh, I really, really, really want to be this character.*

I went in for a pre-read with the casting director, then to a callback, a producer session, and two screen tests. I didn't think I was going to get it because they were looking for a 12-year-old brunette who would look like Teri and I was a 13-year-old blonde. At the screen test they asked, "Are you willing to dye your hair?" And I said, "Yes! Yes! Of course I am!" Now people say I look like Teri and that's a very big compliment. We have similar bodies and pretty similar mannerisms too, which is strange. And Lesley Ann Warren really looks like she could be her mother.

My relationship with my mother is more conventional than the one Julie has with Susan. We're very open with each other but my mom is very motherly. I love that Julie often acts like Susan's mother. It's another dynamic of the show that's different from a lot of other shows, and I think it comes off really well on-screen.

A role reversal can work to the negative side, but on this show it's worked for Susan and Julie. Julie's a good kid. She gets good grades in school. She and her Mom get along well. If you watch a lot of other television shows, the kids don't have that much part in it. On this show, the writers give us each our own individual storylines that have a lot of layers to them. It's really fun to play.

Zealous ZACH YOUNG

THE REJECT WITH A CAUSE

Zach Young is the most troubled of the teens on Wisteria Lane — not that he doesn't have competition. Brooding, moody and mysterious, he is a shy kid who radiates strangeness and insecurity. He wears a side part and wire-rimmed glasses and rarely smiles. But it's easy to be sympathetic to him for two good reasons: He has a strange dad, and he lost his mother at a very young age. Since Mary Alice's death, Zach has seemed unsettled and confused, believing that he accidentally killed his baby sister, Dana. It's revealed later, of course, that he's wrong and his parents have told him lies to cover for their own crime.

Who wouldn't be weird with a childhood like that — believing he was a murderer only to find out that his parents were instead? Zach may be the outcast of the Wisteria Lane teens, but it is not without reason. And he is far braver and stronger than many of his more privileged counterparts who have not had to deal with the family troubles he has. He speaks his mind, marches to the beat of his own drummer, and has little tolerance for the banalities of everyday conversation. He wears his strangeness like a badge of honor, which makes him oddly likeable.

I have three siblings who act. My parents ran a theater company out of San Francisco for many years, and then we moved down to Ventura County and did professional theater there. I had a predisposition toward acting because I was immersed in it from a very young age. I did mainly theater until I was 11 or 12, and moving to L.A. was the next step.

I remember reading the audition piece for *Desperate Housewives* and thinking that it was a movie I was auditioning for because it wasn't written in regular television fashion. I remember thinking it had this really odd undercurrent of weirdness. That was something I thought would be fabulous to play.

BIRTHDAY
AUGUST 21

HOMETOWN
CAMARILLO, CALIFORNIA

Cody Kasch appeared in many plays with the Flying H Group in San Francisco, including *Waiting for Godot, God's Country,* and *The Outsiders,* before relocating to Los Angeles with his family to pursue his career.

His TV work includes *Normal, Ohio, NYPD Blue, The Practice, Boomtown, E.R., Boston Public, Phil of the Future, Nash Bridges, Any Day Now, Martial Law,* and *The Others.* He has appeared in the films *Show & Tell* and *Behind God's Back.*

73

Zach is the most evil character I have ever played and I enjoy it. There are so many places I can go with it. You don't get that a lot on television nowadays where you get to take a character from point A to point B, and all the stuff that's in between. I'm exercising my abilities and getting chops as an actor.

I get recognized sometimes but not as much as anyone else on the show does. The other actors look similar to the characters, but my mannerisms, clothing, and posture are all vastly different from Zach's. Usually it's older women who come up to me. They say, "Oh, you're much cuter than your character."

Zach and I are similar in that we both have dark sides. I think everyone does. There are certain things in everyone's lives that people just choose not to talk about, and we all know those things are there but we don't ask about them because of manners. When a bunch of people get together there are so many different places they can go with the conversation. But it's always formalities: "Nice to see you, blah blah blah." They never really get into anything real. The great thing about Zach is: that's all that he is, and his attitude is, "Take it or leave it." He's straight to the point. No generic hellos and smiles. He is who he is.

If there were an award for "most unhappy teen on Wisteria Lane" Andrew would surely win. A tempestuous troublemaker with an alcohol addiction, a pot habit, a lack of moral conviction and a confused sexuality, Andrew has spent the first season creating problems for his family. When his parents announce their separation, Andrew blames his mother. But after a fight with Rex over whether he can live with him, Andrew drinks too much and accidentally runs over Juanita Solis. While other kids' parents would turn them in to the police, Andrew's parents cover for him. And instead of feeling guilty, he just feels "off the hook."

Andrew is angry at everyone around him, but like most boys he tends to take most of his anger out on his mom. He yells at her, humiliates her in front of George, shoves her, even spits in her face.

It is only after trying unsuccessfully to discipline him on their own that Bree and Rex finally send him to a boot camp for troubled teens. Finally Andrew begins to confront his sexuality, but he is in for quite a ride—his religious mother believes he will go to hell, and tries to scare Andrew straight by quoting the Bible. He pretends to clean up his act, making Bree think he's a good kid, secretly planning a rebellion so great it may destroy her.

> "You're so selfish! You know, I am so looking forward to the day I get to put you in a nursing home."

Andrew and Danielle
VAN DE KAMP
THE THOROUGHLY UNPERFECT KIDS OF A PERFECT MOM

Danielle Van de Kamp is a woman on the verge. Like many teenaged girls, she finds that her mother seems to stand in the way of everything she wants. She dreams of becoming a model but when an opportunity arises, her mother sabotages it. She wants to lose her virginity to John, but gets rejected by him after her mother asks him to dump her (and to be "brutal"). As strong-willed as her mother, she has a hard time taking "no" for an answer, romantically or otherwise, and she will do almost anything to insure that she does not turn out like Bree.

Despite her sarcastic demeanor and her habit of mouthing off to her parents, she loves them and wishes they would stay together.

A typical vain teenager, Danielle has a tendency to brush her hair in the midst of the worst family conflicts and ignores familial strife until it affects her, like when her mother makes the bed before taking Rex to the hospital and she sees firsthand just how unstable Bree really is.

> "Look, Mom, I love you a lot. But you really are the last person to ever give anyone advice about sex and happiness."

SHAWN PYFROM

BIRTHDAY

AUGUST 16

HOMETOWN

LOS ANGELES, CA

Shawn Pyfrom stars in the Disney remake of *The Shaggy Dog*. His television appearances include *7th Heaven*, *Touched by an Angel*, and the ABC Movie of the Week *Come On Get Happy: The Partridge Family Story*. He has had recurring roles on *Still Standing* and *8 Simple Rules*, and has also appeared on *Malcolm in the Middle*, *Reba*, *The Drew Carey Show*, *Buffy the Vampire Slayer*, *LA Doctors*, and *Chicago Hope*. Film credits include *Pay It Forward*, *A Day in the Life*, and *Max Keeble's Big Move*. When not working, Pyfrom enjoys rollerblading, listening to music, hanging out with friends, and going to the movies. He also enjoys volunteering his time with needy children.

JOY LAUREN

BIRTHDAY

OCTOBER 18

HOMETOWN

ATLANTA, GA

Joy Lauren began acting with the Alliance Theatre in Atlanta before moving to Los Angeles at age 11 to pursue her love of acting. Her television work includes *The Division*, *Still Standing*, and *Lizzie Maguire* and she has appeared in the films *Holden*, *Finance Matters*, and *Rogues*, as well as many commercials. Lauren also has a passion for dance. She performed with the Atlanta Dance Company and still takes frequent dance classes. She began riding when she was thirteen and hopes to have her American Saddlebred horse, Thomas, ready for shows next year.

an interview with
SHAWN PYFROM

I like being the bad guy. There aren't a lot of bad guy roles out there for kids my age, unless it's the bully at school, or some sort of cliché. I really like my character. In some ways he's like me—the good parts, but it's fun reaching down into that part that is so narcissistic and evil. I like to think I haven't been as mean to my mom as Andrew has been to Bree, but I'm sure I have. Everyone's had their moments with their family.

I was surprised by the plot turn where Andrew is gay; I was slightly excited to play that. It was something different and interesting that I had never done. And I was really excited with the way Marc Cherry wrote it.

I've had a few people just come up and tell me how much they hate me on the show. I take it as a compliment, because it means I'm doing something right. There are a lot of tough, scary-looking guys that come up to me and recognize me. This guy came up to my car once, this really scary-looking guy, and I didn't know what he was going to do. When he got there he said, "You're on *Desperate Housewives*. I love that show."

an interview with
JOY LAUREN

I saw the sides for the character, and I liked her because she was really sarcastic and almost careless about what's going on inside her family. I can definitely see where Danielle's coming from. Imagine growing up in a house where everything around you is always so perfect. There comes a point where you just say, "This isn't normal. I can't do this any more."

Bree's very determined with everything she does, so in that way Bree and Danielle are a lot alike. I don't think Danielle wants to be like Bree, but part of her will end up that way. People become their parents. It's the cycle of life.

I went to the Family Television Awards and on the press line one of the reporters said, "How can you come to a family television program? You're not on a kid-friendly show." I said, "Family's about knowing what your kids can handle. They can watch it if they can handle it." There are a lot of interesting topics on the show, but it's nothing that's not in other shows that people's kids are watching.

Our series shows a wide selection of different relationships. If you look at Julie and Susan, their relationship is really sweet and they're really close. That's how my mom and I are. And the other families are all different. *Desperate Housewives* shows a lot of dynamics, and it definitely goes to the extremes of those dynamics.

THE LITTLE IMPS

Porter, Preston, Parker, & Penny

SCAVO

x

76

The four Scavo children, Porter, Preston, Parker, and Penny, seem to exist to cause their parents aggravation. Incredibly hyperactive and prone to making trouble, the twins and their brother, Parker, drive Lynette and Tom to the brink. They make fortresses in the living room, throw balls in the house, pull the petals off of flowers, get bubblegum in their hair, catch lice, and generally do all that they can to misbehave. They steal from neighbors, hide out where they shouldn't, run their grocery carts into innocent old ladies. They are loud and incredibly willful and seem to get a perverse charge out of disobeying their mother. Everyone knows kids like this, and every parent feels like they are raising Scavo kids on some days, but few are unlucky

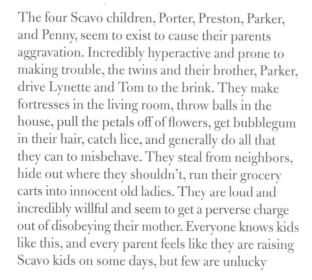

enough to be hit with four of them in six years. As Lynette tries to stay sane in the face of caring for her imps, only one thing comes to mind: *Thank God those aren't my kids.*

SHANE & BRENT KINSMAN

....

BIRTHDAY
NOVEMBER 3

....

HOMETOWN
LOS ANGELES, CALIFORNIA

Twin brothers Brent and Shane Kinsman got their acting break at age four while attending an L.A. Dodgers game, where a talent agent spotted them. Their first booking was a Tylenol commercial. They have also appeared in *Cheaper by the Dozen,* where they were cast as the "identical menaces" of Steve Martin and Bonnie Hunt's family and will appear in the sequel. In their spare time they enjoy playing video games, skateboarding, in-line skating, and dirt bike riding.

ZANE HUETT

....

BIRTHDAY
MAY 9

....

HOMETOWN
RIVERSIDE, CALIFORNIA

Zane has been in several commercials and feature films, including *Just Another Day in the Neighborhood, Daddy Day Care,* and Gregg Araki's *Mysterious Skin.* He loves basketball, baseball, dirt bikes, music, and using his great sense of humor.

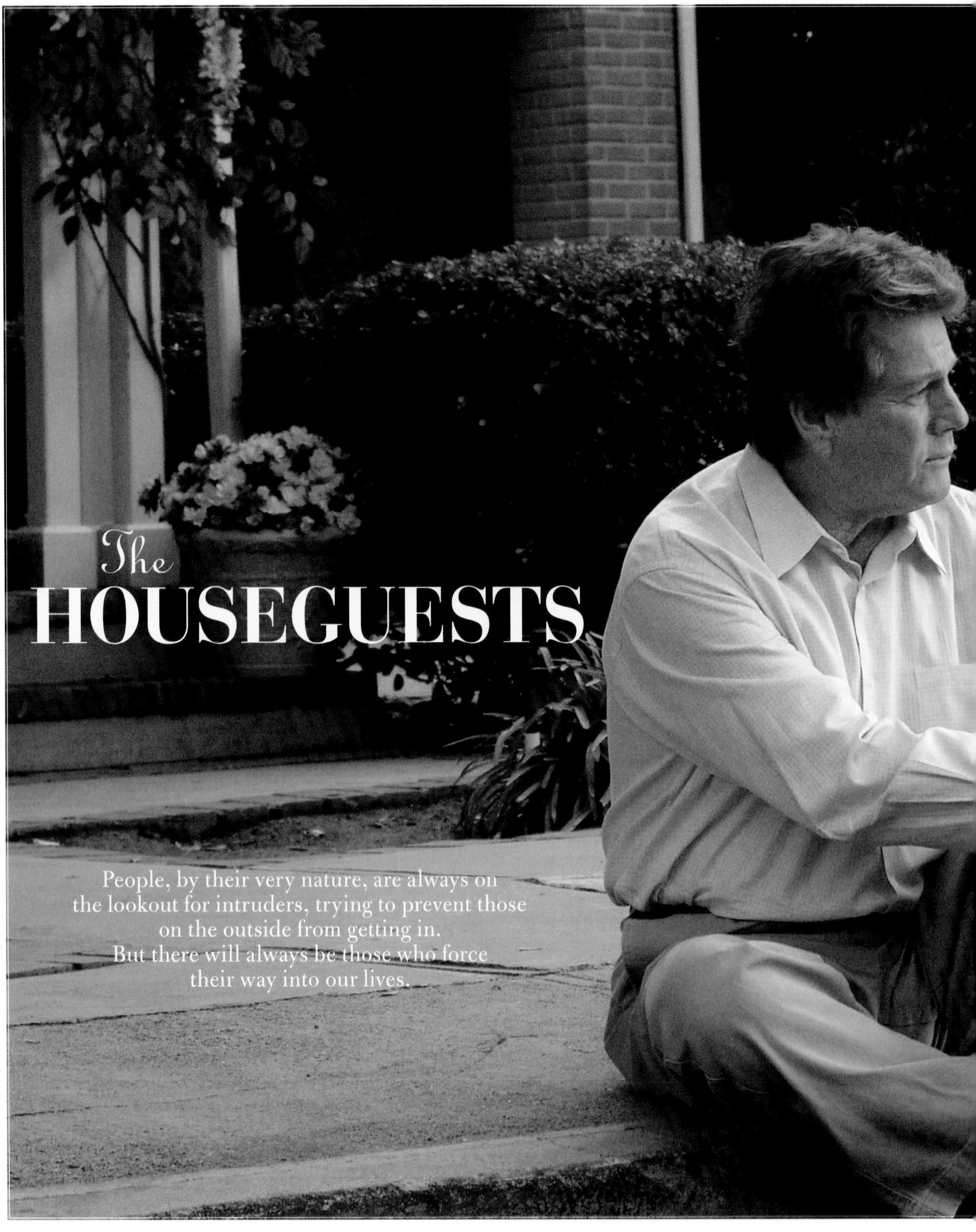

The HOUSEGUESTS

People, by their very nature, are always on
the lookout for intruders, trying to prevent those
on the outside from getting in.
But there will always be those who force
their way into our lives.

FELICIA TILLMAN, *played by* HARRIET SANSOM HARRIS

Mrs. Huber's sister Felicia comes to town to investigate Martha's death and decides not to leave until she finds out what happened. She spots a picture of Mary Alice on Paul's refrigerator and realizes that she knew Mary Alice many years ago in Utah, by her given name, Angela Forrest, and begins to unravel the mystery of "Dana." This woman has a way of holding gardening shears that makes you want to run into the bushes and hide. But as seen in her climactic scene with Paul, her bravado is a cover for a much more vulnerable inner self.

"Don't look shocked, Martha. It makes your face look fat."

Marc Cherry: I worked with Harriet on another show, The Five Mrs. Buchanans. *When I wrote the part of Mrs. Huber, my first choice was Christine Estabrook, who played it, and my second choice was Harriet. In the back of my head, I said, "Well, Mrs. Huber's going to die, and I'm going to need someone to play her sister, so if I get Christine to play Mrs. Huber, Harriet will play her sister." I got it the way I wanted it. Harriet's one of those people who is a consummate professional.*

GEORGE WILLIAMS, *played by* ROGER BART

When Bree first asks out this oddball pharmacist, it is out of a desire to make Rex jealous. But on the date George realizes how much he likes Bree, and when she stops seeing him, he can't stop thinking about her. At night he watches surveillance videos of Bree in the pharmacy and by day he begins to poison her husband by tampering with his medication. Later, he snoops in the Van De Kamp home and finds out how to turn her away from Rex. This obsessed loner may bring Bree more pain—or he just might become her new love interest.

"I've found with the right chemicals you can get rid of almost anything."

Marcia Cross: I love Roger. I think there's something delicious in the combination of George and Bree. In some ways they're both misfits. There's a wavelength on which they understand each other. When I'm working with him I find another color to her, a sensitivity that comes out. I also think that as an actor he's extraordinary. He's so committed.

Marc Cherry: I was scared to death of casting Roger because I knew him from these big, extravagant Broadway musicals, You're a Good Man, Charlie Brown *and* The Producers. *He did a really nice audition on the tape so we went ahead and cast him. And he may very well be one of my top three favorite guest stars of the entire first season, because he's turned out to be so subtle. He plays George as just so deliciously wicked and subtle that it's one of the best pieces of casting we did.*

JUANITA SOLIS, played by LUPÉ ONTIVEROS

Juanita Solis is one of the scariest mothers-in-law to appear on network television. Gaga over her son Carlos, she has been devoted to him since he was a boy and his father, Diego, used to beat him. Juanita has nerves of steel. She is fearless, manipulative, and dogged. At Carlos' request she agrees to trail Gabrielle to see if she's cheating on him and when the poor woman learns the truth, she's hit by a car and goes into a coma. This strong survivor eventually wakes, then falls down a flight of stairs, unable to get the secret out because the hospital nurse had her headphones on.

Eva Longoria: I'm a big fan of Lupé Ontiveros. I grew up watching Lupé in numerous things. She's a Latin icon in the acting world for us Latinos, so to be able to work with her and play her daughter-in-law was just a dream. She's such a wonderful human being. She's heavily involved in Latino civil rights as well so, you know, we've known each other for a while through organizations like the NCLR and MALDEF. You always know people in the industry and you meet people, but to have a chance to work with people that you've admired is an awesome feeling. I wish Juanita didn't die.

> "Family should always hug, regardless of how they feel about each other."

Ricardo Antonio Chavira: Lupé is from El Paso, Texas, so it was great to work with another Tejano. She's got so many stories and so much work experience. She reminded me of all my tias, my aunts, and older cousins. There are so many women I grew up with that used to henpeck me, and tease me. She's like my tia Berta, beer drinking, cussing and smoking cigarettes, just a big heart and full of life. She demands you step up your game when you're doing a scene with her.

81

Marc Cherry: I had seen Lucille Soong in Freaky Friday, *and I thought she would be an interesting addition to our world. I was also trying to bring in as many ethnic faces as possible. At first I wanted a white maid, so that the Hispanic couple had a white maid. But we were going over budget in those first few episodes, and if you cast a person of color, the diversity fund pays for it. So it was also a budgetary decision.*

> "The only reason you have anything in your life is because you're pretty. One day you'll be old. And when that happens, you'll be nothing."

YAO LIN, played by LUCILLE SOONG

Carlos and Gabrielle's maid Yao Lin is the employee from hell. Though she does a good job on the house, she bickers with Gabrielle, is resistant to her demand that she clean with John's striped gym sock, and makes Gabrielle's life miserable. After the Solises finally fire her because of their money problems, Yao Lin runs into Gabrielle at the cosmetic counter where she's working and demands a makeover, the ultimate humiliation.

MAISY GIBBONS, *played by* SHARON LAWRENCE

Marc Cherry: Sharon Lawrence came very close to getting the part of Bree. We ultimately went with Marcia for a variety of reasons, but I loved Sharon Lawrence's take on my words and I knew I wanted to get her on the show. We put her in the part of Maisy Gibbons, the woman who Lynette goes up against, but then we decided to do a house-wife hooker storyline. We were all talking about desperate things we've heard of housewives doing. I thought, Let's have Maisy be revealed as the hooker. It all came out of my love for Sharon Lawrence and her talent.

The neighborhood alpha mom, Maisy Gibbons is June Cleaver crossed with Heidi Fleiss. A bully who treats her fellow school moms like corporate minions, her real profession is turning tricks in her bedroom to help support her family.

"I've been 'abandoned.' I guess that's what happens when you become the town whore."

DR. ALBERT GOLDFINE, *played by* SAM LLOYD

As Bree and Rex's marriage counselor, he tried to be a neutral party to the growing rift between the couple and was the only person who knew about Rex's fetish besides Maisy Gibbons. He was also Mary Alice's shrink and may have been the first person to learn the truth about "Dana."

Marc Cherry: We knew that Rex and Bree were going to have a troubled marriage and we thought a counsel-ing session would be an interesting way to examine some of their stories. I was a big fan of Sam Lloyd from his work on The West Wing *so I said, "Let's go with Sam."*

"Well, as long as you have a plan."

Although Sophie told Susan that Morty assaulted her, this restaurant owner couldn't hurt a fly. Hapless, dogged, and over the moon about Sophie—regardless of her wacky ways—he finally proposes to her, with his dead wife's engagement ring. He has found his one true love, even if it took him more than half his life to do it.

MORTY, played by BOB NEWHART

83

Marc Cherry: Bob was on our wish list for Morty, and when we found out he might be available, my entire writing staff was just over the moon. Morty had to be played by someone who you couldn't believe would actually hit a woman—an actor where, once you saw Morty, you just laughed, and that's why he was perfect. You're always scared to work with your comedic icons because you don't know what they're going to be like in real life and he turned out to be just as nice as you'd imagine Bob Newhart to be.

"I thought I could be happy. I mean, the restaurant is starting to make money, I just bought a new Jet Ski. My cholesterol is down. But none of it is any fun … without her."

Sophie is Susan's mother. A knockout brunette who is obsessed with looking young, she is also a drama queen who tends to exaggerate the truth. Troubled in her relationship with her long-time boyfriend Morty, she asks Susan if she can move in. She tries to arrange double dates, she slows down the ice cream truck to flirt—generally doing everything she can to disrupt her daughter's life. When Morty finally comes back and proposes, Sophie leaves, and Susan just might be a little sad to see her go.

"Tomorrow we'll trade this in for a ring of my own. And I want a bigger diamond than Dolores got."

Marc Cherry: We cast Lesley Ann because she seemed like the Teri Hatcher of the '70s. I've been a fan of hers for years, going back to Victor/Victoria and Cinderella. Getting to work with her was a huge honor.

RODNEY SCAVO, played by RYAN O'NEAL

Tom's father, Rodney, comes for a visit to see the family and Lynette winds up walking in on him with a woman who is not his wife. Rodney's visit spurs a frank conversation between the Scavos about commitment and fidelity. Unknown to Lynette, Tom confesses to his father a secret in his own past, revealing that he may not be the perfect husband.

Marc Cherry: For the role of Tom's father, we originally thought, Let's go get a big star. Ryan O'Neal was at the top of the list, but we were concerned we weren't going to be able to get him due to money and time issues. At the last second, it worked out. I was so glad. One of my little jokes with that part is that I named him Rodney and Tom's mother Allison, and of course, Rodney and Allison were the lead characters in Peyton Place, *played by Ryan O'Neal and Mia Farrow. One of my daydreams is to get Mia Farrow to play Tom's mother for a future story line.*

"My sex life is my own business, not yours. And there's nothing you can do about it anyway."

JUSTIN, played by RYAN CARNES

When Justin offers to mow the Solises' lawn for free, Gabrielle is suspicious, and well she should be. First he tries to demand sexual exchange for keeping quiet about John. But when Gabrielle digs deeper she discovers that he is questioning his sexuality and only wants to make out with her to determine if he is gay. Unsure of his identity, he is beginning to have feelings for this buddy he messes around with sometimes, none other than Andrew Van de Kamp.

"Just so you know, I never would have told Mr. Solis about you and John. I may be gay but I'm not a jerk."

HELEN ROWLAND, *played by* KATHRYN HARROLD

John the gardener's mother first suspects John of having an affair with Susan, but when Gabrielle confesses the truth to her she vows revenge. She chooses not to blackmail her for money (a good idea, since the Solises don't have any), but tries to get Gabrielle to talk John out of his plan to open a gardening business instead of attending college. Gabrielle tries but it doesn't work. John is too in love with her to listen and so instead, he proposes.

"There's a special place in hell for people like you."

"The heart wants what it wants…"

Marc Cherry: Karl was a little hard to cast, because we wanted a guy that was nice looking and seemed like he would have been married to Teri, but was also someone you wouldn't like. When Richard Burgi came in we thought he was just terrific. Another actor played Karl in the pilot but the conception of the part changed a little bit, and we just felt at the end of the day, we needed something a little different.

KARL MAYER, *played by* RICHARD BURGI

Susan's ex-husband and Julie's father, Karl is the ex we love to hate. He left Susan for his secretary, Brandi, who looks like she's Julie's age, and doesn't even have the courage to apologize to Susan for hurting her. Later, at Julie's birthday party, Edie lets it slip that Karl felt her up at a holiday party. Worse, he has the nerve to ask Susan to take him back. Luckily for her, she has the wherewithal to say no.

KENDRA, *played by* HEATHER STEPHENS

"You two just won't stop, will you? Deirdre's dead. It doesn't matter who killed her. Just let it go."

Noah's daughter Kendra comes to pay Mike a visit, sending Susan on a paranoid tailspin that she is more than just a friend. During a scene in a rodeo bar she tells Susan that Mike has secrets, making Susan wonder if there is more to this mysterious plumber than meets the eye.

THE CHARACTER OF DEIRDRE WAS NAMED AFTER WRITER KEVIN MURPHY'S SISTER. THOUGH SHE WAS FLATTERED WHEN SHE FIRST LEARNED OF THE CHARACTER, SHE BECAME LESS ENTHUSED WHEN SHE LEARNED WHAT HAPPENED TO DEIRDRE.

NOAH TAYLOR, *played by* BOB GUNTON

Noah is Deirdre's father, and has hired Mike to find out what happened to her. He pays Mike a small salary to investigate the murder, and when Mike goofs by getting shot in the middle of a break-in, Noah warns him not to make any more mistakes. Noah is a father obsessed with finding out what happened to his daughter. He even goes so far as to bribe the detective when Mike is brought in for questioning in Mrs. Huber's murder — just so Mike can get on with his work. And when he learns that Deirdre has been killed, he weeps for his lost daughter.

Marc Cherry: We named this character Noah, after Noah Cross, John Huston's character in Chinatown. *We knew we needed a heavy hitter for that part, and we were really lucky that Bob Gunton was available. I'm a big fan of Bob Gunton — he was the original Juan Peron in* Evita *and I'm all about musical theater.*

James Denton: Bob Gunton is such an interesting actor, and every take is different. Just watching him, you can get lost in the scene, which is a lot of fun. And we had a really great scene in the graveyard where he's crying about his daughter, and it was really touching. It's also more fun to play a different side of Mike. It's only with Bob that I get to be the real Mike. Noah knows Mike, and he's onto Mike, and Mike's honest with him.

"I'll be dead inside a year. I've got bigger things to worry about than my waistline."

MRS. McCLUSKEY, *played by* KATHRYN JOOSTEN

The Scavos' mean older neighbor, she grows angry when she learns that the boys have been stealing things from her home. She and Lynette keep butting heads, but one day when the boys go over to apologize she tells them about her own son, who died when he was young. It turns out the neighborhood sourpuss has a reason for being the curmudgeon she is and is capable of much greater warmth and depth than Lynette could know. Later, when Mrs. McCluskey's health problems get worse, Lynette finds herself acting as an unlikely benefactor — and even a friend.

"Nobody's ever going to love you like your mother."

Marc Cherry: We were talking about doing a story with a hideous neighbor who doesn't like Lynette's kids and one of the writers came up with the idea that her own children had died, so that's why she's hard on kids. Kathryn Joosten was just a last minute replacement. We had another actress playing the part, and we had to fire her. Kathryn turned out to be spectacular.

MR. SHAW, *played by* RICHARD ROUNDTREE

Paul Young hires Mr. Shaw to kill whoever was blackmailing Mary Alice. Mr. Shaw thinks it is Edie until he learns that her stationery was stolen by Mrs. Huber. He tells Paul the truth and it's not long before Paul takes matters into his own hands. Later, when Susan hires him to figure out what happened to "Dana," this clever PI takes money from Paul and lies to her.

Nicollette Sheridan: I had a love scene with Richard Roundtree that was cut from the show. After he realizes that Edie wasn't the one who wrote that note, he follows her back to her hotel room. Cut to Edie coming out of the bathroom in lingerie, high heels and an Hermès whip saying, "You ready for round three?" She struts across the bedroom and climbs on top of him.

Marc Cherry: We wanted to put an African-American face on the show. Of course, the part was a very dangerous, malevolent guy. But we had a bunch of different actors come in, and Richard Roundtree did a really good job at the audition. Also, he's Richard Roundtree. We shot a hotel room scene between him and Nicollette, but when we saw the scene, it became about how skimpy her underwear was and how great her body is, and it just got to be too much. We were also running long. Before that episode aired, the Monday Night Football *scandal happened, so when people heard we cut the scene they thought it was because of that. But it wasn't.*

"Sometimes evil drives a minivan."

ALISA STEVENS, played by MARLEE MATLIN

Alisa is a deaf parent at the Barcliff Academy who befriends Lynette. After Lynette sees that her husband talks about her badly when she's out of lip-reading range, she meddles. As usual for Mrs. Scavo, the plan backfires, and Alisa's husband leaves her. She signs off with the memorable insult, "Bitch," which needs no translation.

Marc Cherry: Marlee actually called and said she wanted to do the show. That was the very first example of someone calling and saying they wanted to do the show, and me thinking about it and finding a place for them. I thought, Oh, okay, and I got intrigued by the problems of a deaf housewife.

CLAIRE, played by MARLA SOKOLOFF

After her addiction to her kids' ADD medication, Lynette hires this wholesome nanny away from her employer. Lynette finally has relief, until Tom realizes he's attracted to Claire and the Scavos decide she must hit the road.

Marc Cherry: Originally, we were going to do a whole different storyline with a nanny who turns out to be a lesbian and falls in love with Lynette, but she's such a good nanny Lynette doesn't want to let her go. Once we cast Marla and she started shooting the first of her two episodes, we realized that she was so unrelentingly straight that it suddenly seemed false to us. We switched it around so that she was just a normal girl and Tom got a crush on her. We might still do the other storyline in a future season.

Doug Savant: Marla Sokoloff is such a sweet, lovely young lady. She was rightfully demure and was not used to having other characters making comments about her physical being. There are these shots where Tom is ogling her breasts. And when we were shooting it I said, "Well, if you could find a little spot on the table and really rub it, it would cause things to shake a little." She didn't think that was very funny.

THE SIESTA KING CHARLIE SKOURAS, played by JON POLITO

This gravelly voiced mattress salesman hires Gabrielle as a model, but the petulant housewife resents having to lounge around in lingerie on beds all day. She puts up a sign that says DO NOT TALK TO MODEL, and when Charlie finds out he gives her a lecture on how to be a team player. In keeping with her character, Gabrielle is unrepentant, and the Siesta King lets her go with the memorable phrase, "You're fired, Princess."

88

OFFICER RICK THOMPSON, played by STEVEN ECKHOLDT

This friendly neighborhood cop is a better womanizer than detective. Instead of taking the screwdriver Susan finds in Mrs. Frome's house to be dusted for prints, he asks Susan out on a date. She doesn't want to go because of Mike, but when she tells him about the date, Mike takes no interest, so she goes. At first Officer Thompson seems like a nice guy but after Susan challenges him for not running tests on the evidence, he calls her a psycho. Realizing he is just another "Karl in disguise," she wanders off in the middle of the red light district, to be rescued by a definite non-Karl, Mike Delfino.

ASHLEY BUKOWSKI, played by EMILY CHRISTINE

This little girl catches Gabrielle and John kissing. Though she may not yet know how to spell, she instinctively knows how to blackmail, demanding that Gabrielle buy her a bike and then teach her how to ride it.

FATHER CROWLEY, played by JEFF DOUCETTE

This priest knows the truth about Gabrielle and John and tries to get Gabrielle to see the error of her ways. But when he tells her she can repent later, Gabrielle decides to postpone her confession. A level-headed, good priest, he is one of the few people who is honest with Gabrielle, calling her a "selfish child." Instead of bristling, Gabrielle begins to wonder if maybe he is right.

Housewives
IN THE MEDIA

Thanks to the genius of Marc Cherry, and in no small part to the marketing geniuses at ABC, *Desperate Housewives* was an instant hit. Before the pilot was even picked up by the network, the ad department began thinking about how to promote the show, selecting the slogan "Everyone has a little dirty laundry" after determining that the series' primary audience would be women aged 18–49. After an advertising blitz that included women's magazines like *InStyle*, *People*, and millions of dry-cleaning bags, the show won an astounding 21 million viewers for its premiere on October 3, 2004, and kept growing. Although the original ad campaign targeted female viewers, within a month the Nielsen ratings showed that its viewership was forty percent male, proving that the mystery, camp, and comedy were just as appealing to desperate husbands as to desperate housewives.

The show's status as a cultural phenomenon was cemented on November 15, 2004 when, as a lead-in to *Monday Night Football*, ABC Sports aired a racy sketch starring Nicollette Sheridan and Philadelphia Eagles receiver Terrell Owens. After viewers complained, ABC Sports apologized for the segment.

After that brouhaha, which was debated and replayed endlessly on television news, those who hadn't yet tuned in began to take interest — if only to see that smokin' Nicollette Sheridan one more time. *Housewives* became a "water cooler show" that people could discuss on Monday mornings, musing on why Mary Alice might have killed herself or which housewife (or husband) they most resembled. Compared to *Sex and the City* and *Peyton Place*, the show received critical raves that cited everything from its serial storylines to its take on modern motherhood as reasons for its success.

Housewives had become not only a hit show but a bona fide pop-culture phenomenon. The stars began appearing on magazine covers from *Time* to *Entertainment Weekly* to *Ms. Newsweek* ran a cover with the stars in an article called "Has Pop Culture Gone Too Far?"

The show's success coincided with the 2004 Presidential Election, so it was only natural that *New York Times* op-ed columnist Maureen Dowd, just a few weeks after Bush's re-election, wrote, "Trapped in their blue bell jar, drowning in unfulfilled dreams, Democrats are the *Desperate Housewives* of politics."

In May 2005, at the White House Correspondents' Association Dinner, First Lady Laura Bush referenced the show: "At 9 o'clock, Mr. Exciting here is sound asleep and I'm watching *Desperate Housewives* — with Lynne Cheney. Ladies and gentlemen, I am a desperate housewife." Soon the producers began negotiating with her to guest-star in the second season.

A show that began as a gleam in the eye of Marc Cherry was now considering guest spots with the President's wife — and all in the space of seven short months. It was only a matter of time before it would be written up in semiotics books and deconstructed by women's studies majors everywhere.

It is said that parody is the sincerest form of flattery and it wasn't long before the show found itself being spoofed all over TV. **Sesame Street** ran a parody called **"Desperate Houseplants,"** about houseplants that weren't getting enough water and sunlight. Oprah Winfrey visited Wisteria Lane and shot a spoof in which she was the new housewife on the block who moved into the *Munsters* house and then left with her husband after realizing how weird everyone was. At the **TV Land Awards**, just after *Desperate Housewives* won the "Future Classic" award, Eva Longoria introduced a skit called **"Desperate Classic Housewives,"** starring Marion Ross, Barbara Eden, Charo, Joyce DeWitt, and Shirley Jones. And the notorious **MAD Magazine**, known for its hilarious skewers of pop culture, spoofed the show in a parody called **"Disparate No-Lives"** penned by Mort Drucker and David Shayne.

(Marc Cherry was sufficiently amused to include an excerpt in this book. Turn the page.)

1 CHARO The Love Boat **2** JERRY MATHERS Leave It To Beaver **3** ABE VIGODA Barney Miller
4 DON KNOTTS Three's Company **5** MARION ROSS Happy Days **6** TOM BOSLEY Happy Days **7** JOYCE DEWITT Three's Company
8 SHIRLEY JONES The Partridge Family **9** BARBARA EDEN I Dream of Jeannie

It's the number one new drama of the season! Of course, when the competition is *Dr. Vegas* and *Jack and Bobby*, that's like being the smartest kid in the slow class! Still, there must be some reason that tons of folks have been tuning in to ABC on Sunday nights! Let's see, is it...brilliant writing? Nope! Great acting? Nuh-uh! Legions of fans wondering what happened to the dude who played the gay guy on *Melrose Place*? No, probably not! Maybe it's because just like the characters on the show, the audience is made up of a bunch of...

DISPA

RATE NO-LIVES

This is my **clumsy friend Snoozin!** She has a **crush** on our new neighbor **Mock**, but can't **act** on it because she gets so **flustered** around him! **Poor, poor Snoozin!**

Uh, hey, **Mock**, sorry for **running over** your **garbage cans! And** your **dog! And**, uh, your **foot!** Anyway, I thought you might **like** this **apple pie!** Only, I was **out** of **apples**, so I substituted **raw tuna!**

Er…thanks?

Did I say "**Poor, poor Snoozin**"? I meant **poor, poor MOCK!**

My friend **Dinette** gave up her **career** to be a **full-time mom** and she's **never looked back** — mainly because if she **turns** her **head** for even **one millisecond** her **hyper-active sons** will **destroy her!**

Honey, I think we should consider **adoption!**

What? You want **another baby?**

No, I want to **unload** *these* four **monsters!**

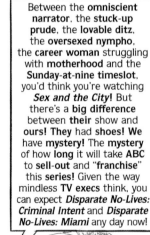

Qt DRUCKER

My friend **Breeze** is **Hysteria Lane's** own little **Martha Stewart** — great **chef**, devoted **homemaker** and **psychotic control freak!**

Hot **muffins**, **fresh** from the **oven!**

But **mom**, I'm **not** hungry!

If you don't **eat** them **right now**, I'll have to **throw** them **away!** And if I do **that**, I'll need to **vacuum** up the **crumbs!** Of course, **THEN** I'll have to **smooth** the **vacuum tracks** out of the **carpet**, in **which case** I might as well get a **new carpet**, and **that** means **new drapes** to **match** and **new wallpaper** and… oh dear, **this** is going to take **all day!**

There's a **betting pool** to see which happens **first: Martha** leaves **jail** or **Breeze** completely **snaps! Martha's term** is **up** in about **six months**, so the **smart money's** on **Breeze!**

Between the **omniscient narrator**, the **stuck-up prude**, the **lovable ditz**, the **oversexed nympho**, the **career woman** struggling with **motherhood** and the **Sunday-at-nine timeslot**, you'd think you're watching *Sex and the City*! But there's a **big difference** between **their** show and **ours! They** had **shoes! We** have **mystery! The mystery** of how **long** it will take **ABC** to **sell-out** and "**franchise**" this **series!** Given the way mindless **TV execs** think, you can expect *Disparate No-Lives: Criminal Intent* and *Disparate No-Lives: Miami* any day now!

ARTIST: MORT DRUCKER   WRITER: DAVID SHAYNE

The
EPISODE GUIDE

Each new day in suburbia
brings with it a new set of lies.
Lies, told not to hurt,
but to make life more pleasant.

When wife and mother Mary Alice Young commits suicide,
her friends Susan, Lynette, Gabrielle, and Bree
are at a loss to explain why. But Mary Alice's death gets them
thinking about the desperation in their own lives.

Episode

THE PILOT

100

96

written by

MARC CHERRY

directed by

CHARLES MCDOUGALL

Susan is just getting over her bitter divorce from her husband, Karl. Lynette, an ad exec turned stay-at-home mom, is dealing with the challenges of raising four young kids with a husband, Tom, who travels a lot. Gabrielle, a former model married to a wealthy businessman, Carlos, is love-starved enough to be having an affair with their 17-year-old gardener, John, and Bree is the perfect wife and mother—in the eyes of everyone but her own family, who feels she has turned into a Stepford mom.

At Mary Alice's wake, Susan meets a handsome plumber named Mike Delfino, but then has to compete with neighborhood vixen Edie Britt for his affections. Rex asks Bree for a divorce, and Carlos is beginning to suspect that John is not doing his gardening. Tom is ignorant about how difficult Lynette's life is, and Mary Alice's widower Paul is acting suspicious—digging something up from the bottom of his pool. When the housewives go through Mary Alice's belongings, they discover a mysterious letter, indicating that Mary Alice was hiding a terrible secret.

"WE ALL HAVE MOMENTS
OF DESPERATION,
BUT IF WE CAN FACE
THEM HEAD ON
THAT'S HOW
WE FIND OUT JUST
HOW STRONG
WE REALLY ARE."

MARC CHERRY: For the character of Edie I wanted to do an homage to the neighborhood slut. I had in mind the character that Kathy Baker played in *Edward Scissorhands*. I did a little tribute to that lineage when Edie is at Mike's house and she says, "I was making ambrosia and I made too much." That was what Kathy Baker brought to the neighborhood barbecue in *Edward Scissorhands*.

GABRIELLE
It's like my grandmother always said: "An erect penis doesn't have a conscience."

LYNETTE
Even the limp ones aren't that ethical.

JULIE
Oh. You mean like how Dad's girlfriend is always smiling and says nice things, but deep down you just know she's a bitch?

SUSAN
I don't like that word, Julie. But yeah, that's a great example.

SUSAN
Oh… I wouldn't eat that if I were you.

MIKE
Why?

SUSAN
I made it. Trust me.

BRENDA STRONG: I came in after Sheryl Lee had already played the role of Mary Alice in the pilot. I think it was a conceptual shift that happened after they cut it together, that they realized they needed something different. There certainly wasn't something wrong with what she did. It was just that instead of vanilla they wanted chocolate, and I happened to be chocolate. When I walked in to audition, Marc Cherry was so sweet. He said, "I hope you don't mind, but I'm going to close my eyes, because I really want to hear how you sound." When I was done with the audition, he opened his eyes and this angelic smile crept across his face, and I thought, Oh, good. Something went right.

EVA LONGORIA: It was really cold when we did the pilot. It was early March and it was freezing. For the scene where Gabrielle mows the lawn in the middle of the party, the grass was wet, and I was in heels, and my dress was lace. It was an old-fashioned lawn mower, so it was hard to push and grass was literally flying up on my face. I remember the director saying, "All that spitting out of the grass, that's great. You should do that." I said, "No. There's really grass in my mouth." "It wasn't hard to act like I was having trouble with the lawn mower because I was. But I thought that the scene was so funny that it was hard for me to keep from laughing.

MARC CHERRY: I had written the scene where Susan makes up a lie about her pipes being clogged to get Mike to come over, and it went out of the draft, but I put it back in for the Susan auditions because I thought it was funny. And Teri did it just beautifully. Later, that moment became the highest testing moment in the pilot, which freaked me out, because I would have thought it would have been one of the bigger comedic set pieces, like burning down the house or the scene in the pool with Lynette and the kids, or Gabrielle mowing the lawn. But it was that: just Susan getting herself in trouble.

MARK MOSES: When we shot the scene where I was digging up the pool, it was three in the morning. I was using a big pick and it kept getting stuck in the meshing. It wasn't a real pool. And then I'd have to pry it out from the chicken wire and bring it up again, knowing they wouldn't be able to use it. Those mistakes happen all the time.

SUSAN: Oh Mary Alice, what did you do?

Episode

AH, BUT UNDERNEATH

101

100

written by
MARC CHERRY

directed by
LARRY SHAW

Gabrielle is distressed that Carlos keeps trying to buy her affection; Bree and Rex begin couples therapy; Susan and Edie war it out for Mike's heart; and Lynette tries tough love with her kids—to disastrous results. Nosy neighbor Mrs. Huber suspects Susan had something to do with Edie's house fire, and Susan debates telling Paul Young about the note. In the middle of the night, he tosses a baby chest into the lake.

CARLOS: When a man buys a woman expensive jewelry, there are many things he may want in return. For future reference, conversation ain't one of 'em.

EVA LONGORIA: I had to hold my breath for a long time in the bathtub scene and I almost drowned. I thought it was a wonderful shot, though, how it seems like she's drowning herself and you hear the voiceover about people wanting life to be over, and then she comes up into the gardener's arms in the bathtub and the voiceover says that Gabrielle found a lifesaver in John.

THE EXPENSIVE ITALIAN MARBLE TABLE GABRIELLE AND JOHN MAKE LOVE ON WAS ACTUALLY MADE OF PLASTER AND WOOD.

101

BREE
We could do it gently. We could tell him about it over coffee and pastry.

LYNETTE
That'll be fun: "Paul, we have proof your wife killed herself over some deep dark secret. Another bear claw?"

MRS. HUBER
Edie, you can be homeless or you can be ungracious. You really can't afford to be both.

JOHN
This is great. I got tons of homework tonight. It's always easier to concentrate after sex.

GABRIELLE
Well, I'm glad I could help. Education is very important.

JESSE METCALFE: For the shot where I fall out of the window naked the stunt guy really had it worse than me. He's the one that flew out the window. They just gave him a little piece of fabric and taped it to his body because they couldn't catch too much underwear as he fell out of the window. All I had to do was stand there. I had a Speedo on under the shirt but Wardrobe kept coming up and tucking it up my butt crack. I had a major Speedo wedgie going on. That was pretty embarrassing.

MARC CHERRY: One review took me to task for having women competing with other women for men. And I thought, *What world do they live in where women don't, especially women over the age of 35?* Every 35-year-old woman I know that's single and is heterosexual is out there looking and getting desperate. As time goes by it gets worse and worse. I think what makes it believable is that Susan doesn't have anyone to talk to so she's made her daughter her surrogate best friend. I thought that was both a real and an interesting characteristic, which let us know, in a subtle way, how lonely this woman was. I borrowed a little from the relationship between Marsha Mason and Quinn Cummings in *The Goodbye Girl* because I thought that was fun.

Episode

PRETTY LITTLE PICTURE

102

written by
OLIVER GOLDSTICK

directed by
ARLENE SANFORD

When the girls realize they were supposed to go to a dinner party at Mary Alice's they decide to hold it anyway, in her honor. Bree, still struggling in her marriage, agrees to host; Susan has tensions with her ex-husband, Karl, and his new girlfriend, Brandi—and winds up baring it all as she bears the burden of her divorce; Gabrielle worries that the little girl next door may have seen her kissing John and is forced to bribe her for silence; and Lynette tries to get Tom to understand what it's like being a full-time mom. Zach finds his mother's revolver and then hears something disturbing on the news about a baby trunk.

LYNETTE: We didn't exactly forget, it's just usually when the hostess dies, the party is off.

MARCIA CROSS: I just didn't want to say that line, "Rex cries after he ejaculates." I thought it was appalling. I went to the reading, and I was going to go in and say, "I can't say this. This is just horrible." And all the men were around the craft services table and they said, "This is the funniest thing." I said, "You're kidding. It's so mean." But when we did the reading, everybody was on the floor. I've never heard anything like it.

DOUG SAVANT: The moment of this episode that I appreciated the most was when Lynette is telling Tom about Rex and Bree and then she says, "Are we happy?" That's what happens in life. Your friends or someone you know goes through a divorce and you reflect that back on your own marriage. Lynette and Tom are people that care deeply about making their marriage work. That reflects a lot of what our viewers go through.

JAMES DENTON: That scene where Susan got locked out naked was a lot of fun. Teri came onto the set in her robe with her tiny little clothing, underwear with the sides cut out, and strategic tape on her chest, opened her robe to the crew, and said, "Here it is! You're going to be looking at it all day! Get used to it!" Everybody laughed and it really broke the tension. After that she never mentioned it. I won't say that the crew didn't have the best day of their lives, but I will say that we didn't talk about it a lot. It was easy to play the part where I find her because in the scene I had to pretend like I was trying not to look at her and that was the actual moment for Teri and me. I think the line of the season is when I walk her home and say, "I wasn't such a gentleman. I kind of peeked." She gets embarrassed and starts to go in, and I say, "For what it's worth... wow." It summed up so much about their relationship.

NICOLLETTE SHERIDAN: When Teri landed in the bushes she got really scratched up. There was blood dripping down her legs. A few days later she showed me what had happened and I couldn't believe that she hadn't been aware of what was going on. I guess her adrenaline just carried her through.

BREE
So, how many will I be cooking for?

GABRIELLE
Seven. Three couples and Susan. Does that sound right?

SUSAN
No, that sounds very, very wrong.

LYNETTE
Clearly there's trouble in paradise.

TOM
Honestly, I'm not that surprised.

LYNETTE
Why not?

TOM
I don't know. I just never got the idea that they were happy.

LYNETTE
Are we happy?

Lynette struggles with whether to put her twins on ADD medication;
Mrs. Huber suspects Susan had something to do with
Edie's house fire—and tries to blackmail her; Carlos thinks Gabrielle is
cheating on him, but winds up roughing up the wrong
guy; and with Rex living at a motel, Bree struggles on her own with
Andrew's rebellious behavior.

Episode

WHO'S THAT WOMAN?

103

written by
**TOM SPEZIALY
& MARC CHERRY**

directed by
JEFF MELMAN

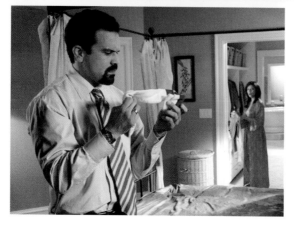

EVA LONGORIA: We were shooting that bathtub scene so long that the stickies on my nipples came off. I didn't realize it. It's such an event for Jesse and me to do nude scenes because we both have so many tattoos and we have to cover all of them. The water turns brown from all the body makeup. Ricardo gets to keep his tattoos because they said Carlos would be a man who had them.

RICARDO ANTONIO CHAVIRA: When the cable guy first comes in the house he makes a comment about the candles Gabrielle is burning. It was a little tip off for later when he turns out to be gay. It's really nice the way the writers plant stuff like that. It's really subtle. They're not slapping you in the face with, "Here's our gay cable guy," but you pick up on something there.

LYNETTE
I used to run a company with eighty-five people and now I can't wrangle three small boys without doping them? Talk about feeling like a failure.

GABRIELLE
Why are your friends staring at me? Did you tell them about us?

JOHN
No, they're staring 'cause they think you're hot.

BREE
Andrew, just because I chose not to share my marital problems with you does not give you the right to be rude.

ANDREW
How about driving my father away? Do I get to be rude then?

105

MARCIA CROSS: I love working with Shawn. He's such a natural amazing talent. He never has a dishonest moment. That scene in the strip club was an out-and-out blast because it was such a different take on that situation. She actually sat there and talked to him about her take on what it was like to be a woman. I think it humiliated him but it wasn't what she set out to do. She was really trying to enlighten him, at least in her mind. Sometimes Bree's not awake to what's happening with him.

"IT WAS COMMON KNOWLEDGE
ON WISTERIA LANE
THAT WHERE SUSAN MAYER
WENT, BAD LUCK
WAS SURE TO FOLLOW."

FROM SEASON TWO ON, ALL EPISODES WILL BE TITLED AFTER STEPHEN SONDHEIM SONGS, BUT IN SEASON ONE SOME EPISODES WERE NAMED AFTER OTHER SONGS. "RUNNING TO STAND STILL" IS A U2 SONG; "COME IN, STRANGER" IS BY JOHNNY CASH; "GUILTY" IS BY BARRY GIBB; AND "ANYTHING YOU CAN DO" IS BY IRVING BERLIN, FROM THE MUSICAL ANNIE, GET YOUR GUN.

106

Episode

COME IN, STRANGER

104

written by
ALEXANDRA CUNNINGHAM

directed by
ARLENE SANFORD

While taking care of her neighbor's dog, Susan and Julie discover evidence
of a break-in, and when Susan tries to get the cop to solve the crime,
he asks her out. Bree gets closer to Zach, who thinks Mary Alice killed herself
because of something he did; Lynette and Tom go overboard
to get their kids into an elite private school; and when Carlos' mother, Mrs. Solis,
comes for a visit, Gabrielle must be more discreet about her affair.
Meanwhile, a mysterious man named Noah tells Mike to be more careful.

JAMES DENTON: Our kiss in Mike's truck was voted by *TV Guide* the eighth hottest screen kiss of all time on TV, which is hilarious for me. Teri was very uncomfortable and very stiff and seemed almost in pain kissing me. I thought, *God, this is not going well. I'm going to get fired.* I found out that she had broken a rib earlier that day on set falling into a wedding cake over and over, and she didn't really tell anybody. Finally they made her go get X-rayed, and it turned out she had cracked her rib. Selfishly, I was happy she had broken her rib, because it had nothing to do with my kissing. Obviously it worked out well for me because I'm still here.

SUSAN: Um, would you repeat that?

SUSAN
It's a shame.
They used to be such
a happy family.

BREE
Just because you didn't
hear them fighting,
doesn't mean they
were happy.

GABRIELLE
For the record,
I am not one of those
women who has
a hole in her heart that
can only be filled
by a baby! I like my life a
lot. It's very fulfilling.

JUANITA
Excuse my
daughter-in-law.
She's very fulfilled.

TOM
Kids in home school
do better in
their later years.

LYNETTE
Why don't we just
put 'em back in me and
cook 'em until
they're civilized?

MARC CHERRY: Susan and Mike's relationship was one I wanted to let develop slowly, but I get bored really quickly so their first kiss happened earlier than it was going to. We've gotten a lot of credit from fans that are used to seeing soap operas that will just drag out story lines ad nauseam. We move pretty quickly on our show. This may come to hurt us down the road, in Season Three when we've used up every possible situation known to mankind, but the fans have enjoyed kind of seeing this romance play out. The scene was written really well. Alexandra Cunningham did such a nice job, and it was just a small but beautifully realized romantic moment.

Gabrielle learns that Mrs. Solis has a gambling addiction and uses the knowledge to get her off her trail; Susan discovers that Paul has checked Zach into a juvenile rehab center; Lynette butts heads with an ubermom who insists on a PC production of *Little Red Riding Hood* — and under the pressure of finishing the costumes for the show, decides to sample her kids' ADD medication; Bree becomes infuriated when Rex suggests they use a sex surrogate, but then tries to seduce Rex in his motel room.

Episode

RUNNING TO STAND STILL

105

written by
TRACEY STERN

directed by
FRED GERBER

LYNETTE: Next spring, we're going to do *Bambi* and his mother is going to take a slug to the head… and you're gonna like it!

EVA LONGORIA: I have a great stunt double. She looks like my twin. I wanted to do the part where I climb over the fence but they said, "We want you to really fly over." I said, "Oh. I can't do that." It was my foot but she was the one who flew over.

JOHN
Danielle?
Oh come on, she's
just a friend.

GABRIELLE
Well, before you get
any friendlier,
let me remind you:
I can do things
to you she can't even
pronounce.

REX
You sound
like a whore.

BREE
No I don't.
I sound like a
woman
whose husband
won't touch her.

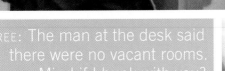

BREE: The man at the desk said there were no vacant rooms. Mind if I bunk with you?

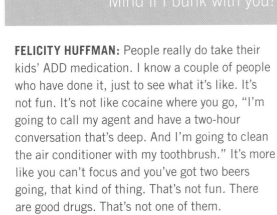

FELICITY HUFFMAN: People really do take their kids' ADD medication. I know a couple of people who have done it, just to see what it's like. It's not fun. It's not like cocaine where you go, "I'm going to call my agent and have a two-hour conversation that's deep. And I'm going to clean the air conditioner with my toothbrush." It's more like you can't focus and you've got two beers going, that kind of thing. That's not fun. There are good drugs. That's not one of them.

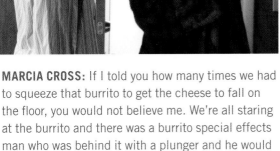

MARCIA CROSS: If I told you how many times we had to squeeze that burrito to get the cheese to fall on the floor, you would not believe me. We're all staring at the burrito and there was a burrito special effects man who was behind it with a plunger and he would push it forward while we were kissing.

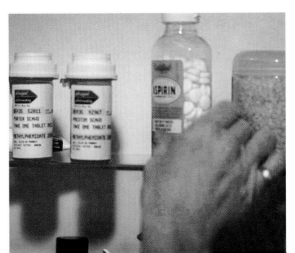

On her way to her first date with Mike, Susan meets his houseguest, a pretty young thing named Kendra, and wonders if they're involved. Mrs. Solis catches Gabrielle and John in the act, takes a picture and then gets hit by Andrew Van de Kamp's car; Rex files for divorce from Bree; and Lynette throws a dinner party for Tom's colleagues. Edie and Susan follow Mike and Kendra to a rodeo bar and Susan gets thrown off the mechanical bull. And the hit man Mr. Shaw becomes convinced that Edie was Mary Alice's blackmailer.

Episode

ANYTHING YOU CAN DO

106

written by
JOHN PARDEE & JOEY MURPHY

directed by
LARRY SHAW

SHAWN PYFROM: When I take the car my dad's bought for me, Marcia was supposed to grab the keys from me and hand them to Steven, and say, "He can't have it." As soon as I got the keys from Steven the keys dropped between the seats. I thought, *Oh shit.* She goes to grab for them, and I say, "I dropped the keys," because I wasn't in the shot. Everyone around us starts laughing, Joy, Steven, the whole crew. But Marcia completely kept it together and pretended she had them. She's amazing.

NICOLLETTE SHERIDAN: When Teri said that line, "FYI," about her date with Mike, I thought Susan was being such a little wench about it that when they turned around on me, I couldn't help but repeat her, "FYI," at the end of it. It stayed in. After that, so many people would come up to me, whenever I was out anywhere, and go, "Oh, we love the show. *FYI.*"

FELICITY HUFFMAN: In the scene where I steal drugs from that medicine cabinet, I had to open the cabinet to look around. It was really late at night when we were shooting and we'd been doing it about a hundred times. Larry Shaw, the director, was saying, "No, you have to grab it from the middle of the shelf," and I was trying to get it right. They called "Action" and when I opened the cabinet there was Larry's big old face going, "Blaaahhhh!" It scared the hell out of me and gave me a lot of energy so I could do it four or five more times.

EDIE: Wow, get a load of you. You look so pretty. I hardly recognize you.

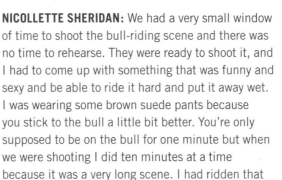

NICOLLETTE SHERIDAN: We had a very small window of time to shoot the bull-riding scene and there was no time to rehearse. They were ready to shoot it, and I had to come up with something that was funny and sexy and be able to ride it hard and put it away wet. I was wearing some brown suede pants because you stick to the bull a little bit better. You're only supposed to be on the bull for one minute but when we were shooting I did ten minutes at a time because it was a very long scene. I had ridden that bull before, up to a ten, which is as high as it goes, and it's never gotten me off.

JULIE
You got protection?

SUSAN
We are so not having this conversation.

JULIE
We are, because I enjoy being an only child.

EDIE
Hey, how was your big date?

SUSAN
Mike had to reschedule.

EDIE
Oh. Because of the hot girl? With the suitcase? Over there? Gosh, how devastating for you. FYI.

ANDREW
Mom, this isn't going to work. I'm not giving up my car.

BREE
That's a smart idea because you're probably going to have to sleep in it for a while.

111

Episode

GUILTY
107

"THERE IS A WIDELY READ BOOK THAT TELLS US EVERYONE IS A SINNER. OF COURSE, NOT EVERYONE FEELS GUILT OVER THE BAD THINGS THEY DO."

FOR THE SCENE WHERE SUSAN FALLS THROUGH MIKE'S BATHROOM FLOOR, THE CREW BUILT A PLATFORM WITH A FAKE HOLE IN THE CEILING. WHEN YOU SEE THE LEGS COME THROUGH THE FLOOR THEY ACTUALLY BELONG TO A STUNTWOMAN WHO WORE BUNGEE CORDS AND A HARNESS.

Susan finds a wad of cash and a gun in Mike's kitchen, winds up snooping when he goes away, and falls through his bathroom floor. With Juanita in a coma, Gabrielle nearly confesses her affair to the local priest, Father Crowley, but decides not to; Bree and Rex leave Andrew's car on Skid Row to hide the evidence; Lynette, hooked on the ADD medication, fantasizes about suicide and breaks down on a soccer field. After Mr. Shaw tells Paul that the blackmailer is Mrs. Huber, Paul murders her himself.

written by
KEVIN MURPHY

directed by
FRED GERBER

ANDREA BOWEN: Susan is going away for the weekend with Mike and she's holding up a shirt to put on. I say, "Oh no, that makes you look old." In one of the takes, I didn't even realize it, but I said, "No, Mom, that makes you look ugly." Teri just stopped and said, "Wait a minute, did you say I was ugly?" We were laughing about that and she said, "I can't believe I'm old and ugly." We went on and got some good takes and then the director comes over and whispers in my ear, "On the next take, say, 'That makes you look a little heavy.'" So on the next take I said it and Teri said, "What? I'm old, ugly *and* fat now?"

113

MARK MOSES: The murder scene with Christine Estabrook, who is a friend, was fun. In between takes she would make faces and gag, "I'm still alive! I don't want to leave the show!" I maintain that Paul Young did not go in there to kill her. He wanted to know why she did this to Mary Alice, which was haunting him, and he found this completely remorseless woman who not only didn't really care about what she did, but then insinuated that his wife was a bad person. And that pushed him over the edge.

FELICITY HUFFMAN: Lynette was supposed to break down at the line, "I love my kids so much, I'm sorry they have me as a mother," but I felt that she had already resigned herself to the fact that she's a terrible mother. What gets to her, and where I decided to lose it, was when the women say they've had the same feelings. It's not the pain of motherhood that breaks her up. It's the release of realizing, *Oh my God. I'm not alone.* For that whole episode, I was very impressed with the producers and ABC for being willing to go dark and ugly early. People tell me they cried when they watched that scene.

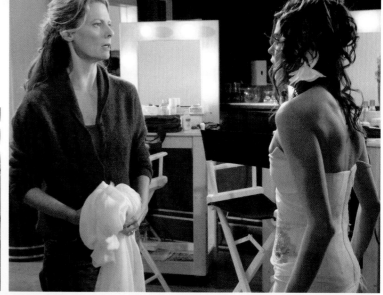

114

Episode

SUSPICIOUS MINDS

108

written by
JENNA BANS

directed by
LARRY SHAW

A repentant Gabrielle decides to put on a charity fashion show to raise money for nurses; Susan discovers Gabrielle's affair and chastises her for betraying her husband; Bree finds marijuana in Andrew's locker and tips off the school; Lynette uses her business savvy to seduce a nanny, Claire, away from her boss; the feds arrest Carlos for unfair business practices; and Zach, who is hiding in Julie's room, confesses that he killed his baby sister, Dana.

STEVEN CULP: When I read the scene where Bree throws urine on Rex I went to Marc and said, "Look, I'm really trying hard not to be just a one-dimensional foil for Bree and it's hard enough without having piss thrown on me." He explained that he didn't want it to be a bad joke on Rex. We talked about what the moment was about and that it was an intense moment between these people. My wife actually gasped when she saw it. The moment was funny but it had all this intense stuff in it.

NICOLLETTE SHERIDAN: I don't know where I came up with that model's walk, or, rather, how Edie would do a model's walk. We had to reshoot it because the first time I came out everyone just started laughing. I did a pony thing. I decided I wanted to be a prancing pony coming down the runway.

HELEN
You remember what it was like dating teenage boys.

GABRIELLE
Vaguely.

EDIE
Can you tell I'm not wearing any underwear?

GABRIELLE
Yes.

EDIE
Good.

BREE
I'm his mother. He lived inside of me!

REX
He hung out in your womb for a few months back in the eighties. Since then, I have grown to love him as much as you.

115

ANDREA BOWEN: I was happy when I found out that Julie was going to hide Zach in her house. I thought, *I get to have a really cool storyline where I get to have some secrets now.* Julie was pretty open and she wasn't hiding anything, so it was fun to be one of the ones with a secret on the show. I'm thinking by the time the show ends, I'll be a desperate housewife.

ZACH: I couldn't remember this for the longest time, and then my mom killed herself and I started having dreams. I don't even see Dana. I just see the blood and my mom picking me up and putting me on my bed and whispering that it wasn't my fault.

Episode

COME BACK TO ME
109

116

written by
PATTY LIN

directed by
FRED GERBER

Susan invites Mike over for a rendezvous and finds that Zach has been hiding in her house; Carlos tells Gabrielle to burn his secret papers and instead she burns his passport so he can't get out; Rex has a heart attack while in a session with Maisy Gibbons — and Bree, thinking they were having an affair, promises to get a lawyer and eviscerate him; and Lynette uses a NannyCam on Claire and learns that even a great nanny can't control her kids.

"TRUST IS A FRAGILE THING.
ONCE EARNED, IT AFFORDS US TREMENDOUS
FREEDOM, BUT ONCE TRUST
IS LOST IT CAN BE IMPOSSIBLE TO RECOVER."

SUSAN
Damn Karl!
I'm not even married
to him any more
and he's still keeping
me from having sex!

· · · · · · · · · · · · · · · · ·

MAISY
Trust me on this.
Sometimes when you
love somebody,
you just
gotta make sacrifices
for them.

REX
Love or passion.
That's an awful choice
to make.

· · · · · · · · · · · · · · · · ·

PAUL
Sometimes it's
not good to look back
on the past.

ZACH
But I can't help it.
These images just keep
popping into my head.

PAUL
Well then you've got
to find a way to push
them back out again.

ZACH
Okay.

PAUL
More potatoes?

· · · · · · · · · · · · · · · · ·

BREE
You are pretty brazen
for a woman who
just admitted, however
tacitly, that she just
slept with my husband.
If I told anyone
in this neighborhood,
they would never speak
to you again.

MAISY
You're not going
to tell a soul.
You may hate me,
but you'd hate
the humiliation a
lot more.

MARC CHERRY: Mark Moses had a scene where he was so happy Zach was home from the mental institution, and he's asking his son if he wants potatoes. It was this twisted Norman Rockwell—esque scene. In the audition, Mark and Cody pulled those lines off beautifully. As a writer, it's nice when you envision something in your head, and it comes back just exactly the way you saw it. Any time Mark and Cody have scenes together I know that they know instinctively how to interpret my stuff.

BREE: Why don't you just call your mystery woman and invite her over? I'll pull out the sofa bed and you can take her right there. Andrew! Danielle! Daddy's going to fornicate for us!

STEVEN CULP: We did two versions of that S&M scene, one that was a little darker and a little edgier, and one where we didn't really see any paraphernalia. Rex and Maisy are having this conversation and ultimately, she starts tying him to the bed. A couple of weeks later, we shot the scene again and it was much better. We're having a conversation about what's going on with the kids and the family, as she's handling all this weird paraphernalia. When I watched it I thought, *God, they're so sad and lost about this.* He's confiding in her. He can't tell his wife about this fetish and he obviously loves his wife. It was sadder than I thought it was going to be.

117

LARRY SHAW: This episode had already been directed and the Rex and Maisy scene wasn't working so we did it again. We couldn't really show sexual toys so I had to bring in unidentifiable medical instruments of some kind. We found this one weird long pointy metal thing that absolutely meant nothing at all. And we thought, *This is so strange looking that no one will ever tell us not to do it.* We started the scene with her pulling it out of a drawer and then I panned up with it up to her and revealed him through the mirror on his knees but it didn't get by Standards and Practices. It was too weird for everybody.

"WE ARE ALL SEARCHING FOR SOMEONE, THAT SPECIAL PERSON
WHO WILL PROVIDE US WITH WHAT'S MISSING IN OUR LIVES;
SOMEONE WHO CAN OFFER COMPANIONSHIP OR ASSISTANCE OR SECURITY.
AND SOMETIMES IF WE SEARCH VERY HARD WE CAN FIND SOMEONE
WHO PROVIDES US WITH ALL THREE."

ORIGINALLY PAUL WAS GOING TO BURY MRS. HUBER ALIVE, SO SHE COULD COME BACK IN A FUTURE EPISODE. LATER THEY CHANGED IT TO HAVING HER HIT WITH A BLENDER AND STRANGLED WITH AN ELECTRICAL CORD, BUT THE WRITERS TOLD ACTRESS CHRISTINE ESTABROOK SHE COULD STILL BE ALIVE. WHEN THE NETWORK DECIDED THAT WAS TOO UNBELIEVABLE THEY DECIDED TO HAVE HER CREMATED, LEAVING

118

Episode

MOVE ON
110

written by
DAVID SCHULNER

directed by
JOHN COLES

Mike tells Susan he thinks she's still got feelings for Karl;
Gabrielle begins modeling to help pay the bills;
Bree, seeking revenge on Rex, asks the local pharmacist
George out on a date; Tom accidentally catches Claire nude;
Mrs. Huber's sister, Felicia Tillman, tells Edie she
believes she was murdered; and Paul removes Mrs. Huber's
jewelry and plants it in Mike's house.

EVA LONGORIA: That scene in the mall was my favorite because the show had just hit and all the fans were there. It was really cool to have all these people watch us shoot. Now it's impossible to do that, but I loved the physical comedy of that scene, getting stuck on the turntable, and I love the actress who played the woman who fixes it. We have a lot of unsung heroes on the show—all the day players and all the guest stars. Our casting directors are amazing because they always pick these wonderful people, who make us funnier.

NICOLLETTE SHERIDAN: We shot Julie's birthday party in a piano bar and I was petrified to sing. Singing in public is not something that I really like to do. Somebody else actually sang the song and I lip-synched but when you lip synch you have to sing it out loud. I thought that I was far away enough from everybody, that they wouldn't be able to hear me. And to my horror, after I finished, they all said that they could hear me and that I was a good singer. But it was mortifying.

BREE: It's a romantic date with a single, attractive man and I intend to French the hell out of him.

STEVEN CULP: It was so much fun to shoot the scene where George picks up Bree for their date. We're such a great team, the three of us. I actually did a couple of rehearsals with the director where he just told us, "Do it really fast." It felt like we were doing some Howard Hawks movie, like Cary Grant and Irene Dunne. We ended up slowing it down but it was great to do it like one of those comedies because it made it less precious. We were just having a good time.

EDIE
Look, Felicia,
it's natural to freak out
when a loved one
is missing.

FELICIA
Loved one?
Oh, Edie, let me be clear
about this.
I hated Martha. She was
a wretched pig of
a woman, and the day
she died, this world
became a better place.

GABRIELLE
You don't think she's...?

SUSAN
Oh no.
I'm sure she's fine.
We're talking about
Mrs. Huber.
She's like a roach.

MICKEY
Look, honey.
I'm the only modeling
agent in a
hundred-mile radius.
I book women for
boat shows and
garden tool expos.
If you don't like it,
move back to the city.

GABRIELLE
This Buick thing—
does it include lunch?

BREE
Yes, I'm angry with him.
I may divorce him.
I may even marry
somebody else.
But make no mistake,
your father is
and always will be
the love of my life.
He gave me the best
eighteen-year
marriage that I could
have ever hoped for.
And for that
you will respect him.

Episode

EVERY DAY A LITTLE DEATH
111

120

written by
CHRIS BLACK

directed by
DAVID GROSSMAN

Susan confesses to Edie that she burned down her house; Carlos, on house arrest, begins tampering with Gabrielle's birth control pills; Bree and George grow closer but on a date to a target range she accidentally shoots him; Lynette manipulates the truth to get into a competitive yoga class; and Noah takes back his money, telling Mike he's moving too slowly.

THE PLOTLINE WHERE PRESTON GETS BUBBLE GUM STUCK IN HIS HAIR CAME FROM MARC CHERRY'S LIFE—HIS SISTER MARCY GOT GUM STUCK IN HER HAIR, AND CHERRY AND HIS SISTER MEGAN GAVE HER AN AWFUL HAIRCUT TO GET IT OUT.

GEORGE: I've always dreamed that before I died I would get to kiss a truly beautiful woman. I finally get the chance and I end up blowing off a toe.

NICOLLETTE SHERIDAN: We had fun shooting that scene where I throw the ashes in Susan's face. Teri was such a good sport. The ash was really cornstarch and we could only do one take because otherwise it would have taken ages to redo her hair and makeup. When I threw it the first time it didn't cover her well enough, so I had to do a double wallop. Teri got some in her eye because she is extremely accident-prone. Then I had to hose her down. At the end of the scene, I just wanted to give her a big hug and say, "I'm sorry." That happens quite often in our scenes.

MARCIA CROSS: I've never shot a gun in real life but I totally committed to it. I love that Bree's an expert in that area. When she's getting the gun from Roger I substituted something that I wanted in my personal life because I couldn't get it up for having a gun. I was actually imagining it was a baby.

RICARDO ANTONIO CHAVIRA: It was amazing to see someone who looks like Eva pigging out on camera. We get to see a beautiful woman eating junk food. On camera—hell, off camera—that's all she does is eat. She's just like a little furnace. I have no idea how she stays in shape because all she does is eat. If I ate that much I'd be 240 pounds.

LAUREN
If I broke the rules for you I'd have to break them for other moms, too, and then the moms who actually followed the rules would get all pissed at me and then I have to get pissy right back, and before you know it I don't have time to read my magazine. See how that works?

LYNETTE
I hope someday you have lots of children.

FELICIA
Look at them all. Vultures. Pretending to care when all they really want are the sordid details.

DETECTIVE COPELAND
I don't know. I think they just want to show their support.

FELICIA
Please. Human beings feed on misery.

LYNETTE
I remember talking to her right before she disappeared.

SUSAN
You did? What did you talk about?

LYNETTE
Oh, actually, she yelled at me for not bringing my garbage cans in.

BREE
I'm gonna miss her.

"SUBURBIA IS A PLACE FILLED WITH RESPONSIBLE PEOPLE TRYING TO LIVE RESPONSIBLE LIVES. OF COURSE, EVEN THE MOST RESPONSIBLE AMONG US HAS MISTAKES IN THEIR PAST, MISTAKES THEY'D LIKE TO FORGET, MISTAKES THAT SOMETIMES COME BACK TO HAUNT THEM."

Susan, infuriated to find Zach and Julie kissing, tries to learn more about Dana from Paul; John's parents tell Gabrielle they won't tell the police about the affair if she tries to talk him into going to college; Bree agrees to give her marriage more time but keeps dating George; George begins tampering with Rex's heart medication; and Tom's father, Rodney, comes to visit.

written by
KEVIN ETTEN

directed by
ARLENE SANFORD

ZACH: You don't care about me! And you didn't care about Mom! You know what? I wish she'd shot you instead!

ANDREA BOWEN: That kiss with Zach was my first onscreen kiss. You show up and you're rehearsing the scene where you're kissing and it's awkward because you have all these people standing around watching you. And your mom is there, so it's strange. But as long as you're acting with somebody who treats it as just any other scene then it takes the weird feeling away. Cody and I pretty much treated it like it was any other scene, so it worked better. We rehearsed the kiss a little and then we were ready to do it on screen.

FELICITY HUFFMAN: When I found out Ryan O'Neal was going to play Tom's father I was shocked. Ryan O'Neal was huge. He was Warren Beatty. He was Tom Cruise. And you hear stories about him, and his daughter wrote the book, so I expected *The Portrait of Dorian Gray*. He showed up and he's this movie star–handsome guy with a twinkle in his eye that's totally charming and loves to talk. I fell under his spell. The thing about acting is, you can't deny what's true. If you find Ryan O'Neal charming, the audience will find Ryan O'Neal charming. That's what I went with for our scene.

GABRIELLE: Every once in a while, even *I* want to do the right thing.

DOUG SAVANT: I loved being able to play that moment where I admitted to my father I did something wrong. People's interest was piqued, but then, just like life, it was dropped. People hold onto their secrets. I don't even think Tom told the whole story to his dad. Probably after the camera went off them, his father said something like, "I understand, but you're going to get through it, and that's that." The Scavos were not a family where communication was key.

SUSAN
Were you just kissing my daughter?

ZACH
Uh, a little.

SUSAN
JULIE
Mom, calm down.

SUSAN
She's only fourteen!

ZACH
Yeah. I should probably be going.

SUSAN
Ya think?

REX
You take our timeshare in Aspen and *I'm* vindictive? Come on. You're hardly ever going to use that place.

BREE
Hardly? How about never?

REX
Fine. When I move out, I'm going to use your good china for takeout food. Yeah. Pizza. Spare ribs.

GEORGE
Is he a good person?

BREE
Aside from the adultery? Yes.

LYNETTE
I made you a drink.

TOM
Oh God. What did he do?

GABRIELLE
I've tried poor but happy. Guess what? I wasn't that happy.

123

"LONG AFTER WE'RE GONE, LOVE REMAINS, BURNED INTO
OUR MEMORIES. WE ALL SEARCH FOR LOVE.
BUT SOME OF US — AFTER WE'VE FOUND IT — WISH WE HADN'T"

Episode

LOVE IS IN THE AIR

113

124

Susan and Mike go on a romantic Valentine's date, where Mike silently bleeds from a shot wound; Gabrielle has to take a job modeling on mattresses and gets fired for insolence; Lynette gets into a war with her irascible elderly neighbor Mrs. McCluskey; Bree confronts Rex about his sexual secret; and Felicia sees a photo of Mary Alice at Paul's house and recognizes her as an old friend, Angela Forrest. Lynette's kids find Mrs. Huber's jewelry in Mike's garage and when she gives it to Susan, Susan thinks Mike had something to do with Mary Alice's murder.

written by
TOM SPEZIALY

directed by
JEFF MELMAN

MARC CHERRY: I wanted Rex to have a sexual secret, and I went back and forth on what it was. At first, I was thinking he might be gay. But I thought, *Well, that's exactly like* Far from Heaven. Marcia's a redhead, just like Julianne Moore. One of the writers came up with the idea that Rex only liked to have sex in filthy surroundings. I toyed with that one for about a day. But I didn't want it to be so bizarre that we couldn't come back from it. So I thought, *How about some nice garden-variety S&M?* I kept waiting for people to be shocked about it, but I haven't heard anything about it. I've gotten a lot more grief over the fact that Gabrielle was having sex with an underage gardener.

125

STEVEN CULP: This episode had a great line that had to be cut. I don't think it got by ABC. Rex says something along the lines of, "I want to be dominated." Bree says, "Huh?" He says, "I want to be dominated, sexually." She says, "Well, I can get on top, just as long as I wear my bra." It was really funny but I don't think they were able to get it past Standards and Practices.

FELICITY HUFFMAN: I found the final moment of this episode really touching. Kathryn Joosten really acted the hell out of it. There's a voiceover at the end, something like, "We don't tell people what we really feel about them." I like that the audience got in on how Mrs. McCluskey had lost her son, and Lynette didn't. It makes them closer to the story. You want to take care of Mrs. McCluskey because inside, you're going, *Oh, if only Lynette knew this, she would be kinder to her neighbor.* But you know she'll never know.

LYNETTE: Are you sure you didn't misplace it? No offense, but you're getting up there in years.

ACTRESS KATHRYN JOOSTEN (MRS. MCCLUSKEY) IS WELL KNOWN FOR HER ROLE AS MRS. LANDINGHAM, PRESIDENT BARTLETT'S ASSISTANT ON *THE WEST WING.*

"BREE VAN DE KAMP BELIEVED IN OLD-FASHIONED VALUES, THINGS LIKE RESPECT FOR GOD, THE IMPORTANCE OF FAMILY, AND LOVE OF COUNTRY. IN FACT, BREE BELIEVED SO STRONGLY IN HER VALUES IT WAS ALWAYS A SHOCK WHENEVER SHE WAS CONFRONTED WITH THOSE WHO DIDN'T."

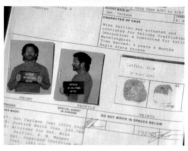

Mike is arrested for Mrs. Huber's murder and Susan finds out that he has been convicted of drug trafficking and manslaughter; Zach throws a pool party and invites the local kids; a new gardener, Justin, demands sex from Gabrielle or he will tell the truth about her affair; Bree finds a condom and learns that Danielle is planning to sleep with John, goes to him and tells him to break it off; Tom is offered a promotion and Lynette insures he doesn't get it; and Noah bribes a detective so Mike will be released from jail.

written by
TOM SPEZIALY & MARC CHERRY

directed by
LARRY SHAW

TERI HATCHER: In that scene where I go from crying about Mike to discovering the two boys making out in the pool, it was a really wonderful example of how well the writers write feelings from anger to tears to tripping over lawn furniture. I am so impressed that they could envision and execute such a great scene.

EVA LONGORIA: It's so exciting to play the scenes where Gabrielle shows more depth. I didn't want to be just the hussy on the show, who is superficial and doesn't have any depth. So once these scenes started to come about, like the speech with Carlos when they're broke and she says, "Poor is just a state of mind," you get to see that vulnerable side of her. It's always nice to see those moments because then you realize she's human.

GABRIELLE: My husband is home quite a lot these days. If any bush needs trimming, he takes care of it.

SHAWN PYFROM: That one kissing scene in the pool took all night. We had to do a lot more than what they used in the episode. I thought, *Damn it, why couldn't they show me making out with him, because I had to do it.* Apparently on network television there have been about twenty scenes of girls kissing girls but only four between guys, and we were one of the four. The actor playing Justin was 23. And he had done it before in another project, so he made me feel as comfortable as you can feel kissing a guy. He was a good actor. When I told my girlfriend about the scene, she said, "I'd rather have you kissing a girl than a guy." But then she saw the guy, and she said, "Oh my God, I wish *I* got to kiss him."

BREE
I know my daughter.
She's very determined.
And unless you're
really firm with her,
she's going to
continue to think that
there's hope.

JOHN
Okay,
I'll be firm.

BREE
Better still,
be brutal.

127

SUSAN: How could you? God. "Susan, do you trust me?" "Yes, of course I do." Oh, I'm such an idiot! And you're such a liar. Oh, and apparently a killer and a drug dealer. That's just quite a personal ad you've got going there.

LARRY SHAW: Before Teri came in to shoot that pool scene I moved all the lawn chairs in a rough way, figuring we'd do something with it. I moved one so close to the edge she had to tiptoe by it and then she had a little gag where she had to get hooked up on underwear with her foot and she had to flip it off her foot without looking at it. Teri did it over and over so perfectly. She's a fabulous physical comedienne. I get the impression from talking to her that this show gives her a real chance to do these things she's good at, but doesn't always have an opportunity to do. It reminds me of Diane Keaton, how she can be so many different colors all at once—confused, knowing, sexy, and out of control.

"EVERYONE LOVES A SCANDAL, NO MATTER
HOW BIG OR SMALL. AFTER ALL,
WHAT COULD BE MORE ENTERTAINING THAN
WATCHING THE DOWNFALL OF THE HIGH
AND MIGHTY?"

After Maisy Gibbons is arrested for
prostitution, Bree tries to bribe
her to remove Rex's name from the black
book; Carlos and Gabrielle, still struggling
with money, have a sewage disaster;
Susan, heartbroken over Mike, goes out and
gets drunk with Edie, after which they
break into Paul's house and find a video of
Mary Alice; and after an outbreak
of lice at the Barcliff Academy, Lynette's
kids are accused of contaminating
the school. Paul tries, not too successfully,
to convince Felicia that Mike was
Mrs. Huber's murderer.

HOUSEWIVES EXECUTIVE PRODUCER CHARLES PRATT JR. WAS ALSO A WRITER ON MELROSE PLACE, WHICH STARRED MARCIA CROSS AND DOUG SAVANT.

128

written by
ALEXANDRA CUNNINGHAM

directed by
ARLENE SANFORD

JAMES DENTON: After Mike's arrested he's trying to win Susan over, and she's resisting, trying to explain to her what happened. She's having none of it, and he just grabs her and kisses her, which is always the right choice. It's like Aunt Eller tells Curly in *Oklahoma,* "Just grab her and kiss her when she acts that way." That was a really great scene.

MARK MOSES: When Nicollette and I were shooting that kissing scene, we were really doing it by the numbers. Scenes like that are like choreography. Before one take, Nicollette arched her eyebrows and just gave me a sexy look. She was trying to say, "You're trying to get it all right, but let's just have a little fun." She was right. I thought, *This* is *fun. I get to kiss Nicollette Sheridan.* That's what was going through my head on the next take.

NICOLLETTE SHERIDAN: There was a scene we shot for this episode that never aired. Gabrielle's thinking about selling the house because she needs the money so Edie goes over to look at it, and she says, "Have the walls always been this orange? Don't get me wrong. I like the color. It's just very… ethnic." At the end of the scene Gabrielle tries to convince Edie she's not selling the house because she needs the money and Edie says, "Honey, you either sell your house because you're moving up or you're moving down. So this is evidence you're moving down." And Edie wipes the banister with her hand and said, "Ooh, your maid needs a slap in the face, doesn't she?"

> **SUSAN:** Every time we went out for pizza you could have said, "Oh, and by the way, I once killed a man." Or when you said, "Hey, let's go jogging," you could have said, "Wow, by the way, I once killed a man." Every time we went to the movies and the hero shot the bad guy you could have turned to me and said, "Oh, by the way, I did that once." You didn't!

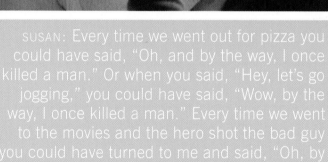

ANDREA BOWEN: There was a part that they cut, where Susan's upset about Mike, and after I leave the room, she just dissolves into tears. Then I come back in and say, "I forgot my magazine," and because Susan doesn't want Julie to see her crying, she sticks her head in the freezer like she's looking for something and says, "I think it's on the table." Then I leave and she takes her head out of the freezer and she's got frozen tears on her face.

LYNETTE
I don't get it. I don't get who would pay Maisy for sex.

GABRIELLE
Obviously someone who's not getting it at home.

EDIE
That's the only nice thing I can say about my first husband. He taught me how to bluff.

LYNETTE
He played poker?

EDIE
No. He was lousy in bed. I had to fake a lot of orgasms.

REX
Everybody's staring, Bree. It's humiliating.

BREE
Well, you should have thought of that before you left a personal check on Maisy Gibbons's nightstand.

129

MIKE
You can't believe I'm some cold-blooded killer.

SUSAN
No. Of course I don't believe that. But I also didn't believe that Karl was going to cheat on me, and I didn't believe that Mary Alice was going to kill herself. I mean, let's face it, Mike. Blind faith is not my friend.

Juanita awakens from her coma determined to tell Carlos about Gabrielle's infidelity, but dies after she falls down a flight of stairs. Mike gives Susan a letter that he says will explain everything but she returns it unread. She agrees to a date with Edie's new contractor Bill even after Edie tells her not to go out with him, and when Edie finds out she tells her, "I will hate you forever." Carlos and Gabrielle argue over funeral costs and then the hospital offers Gabrielle a seven-figure sum as a negligence settlement; Bree and Rex send the troubled Andrew to juvenile boot camp; and Lynette befriends a deaf woman at the Barcliff Academy.

Episode

THERE WON'T BE TRUMPETS
116

written by
**JOHN PARDEE
& JOEY MURPHY**

directed by
JEFF MELMAN

FELICITY HUFFMAN: Marlee Matlin is a fantastic woman who is both really feminine and really ballsy at the same time. She's a mother of four and really honest and doesn't buy into that whole, "Everything's fantastic. I'm the most superb person in the universe. It's not hard" thing. She said, "Yeah, it's really hard." Also, I love episodes where we get to play sports, so the tennis scene was a kick. I can play a little tennis. There was one shot where I had to B-line it at him, and I thought I couldn't do it, so a couple of the crew guys came up and tried it and they couldn't do it at all. I took the racket back and I went, "I can do this." I slammed it right into the camera.

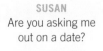

SUSAN
Are you asking me
out on a date?

BILL
Sounds kinda formal
for a burrito and
a can of soda, but yeah,
I guess I am.

SUSAN
Aren't you dating Edie?

BILL
We went out on a date.
We're not dating.

SUSAN
Oh.

BILL
So how about it?
I'm buying.

SUSAN
I just got out of this
relationship with this guy
Mike, and it's kinda
complicated. Anyway,
I'm just not even
sure where I am right
now emotionally.
I'm just all jumbled,
and I don't think
I can leap right into
something new,
relationship-wise, you
know, at the moment.

131

BILL
Again, just a burrito.

LYNETTE
Tom, am I a bad person?

TOM
No. Why would you
say that?

LYNETTE
I don't know.
I guess I just have it
in my head that only bad
people break up
marriages and offend
the handicapped.

MARC CHERRY: I had read about those boot camps for years, and I was very much intrigued by that subject. I had read about this experience where some strange men show up in the middle of the night and just cart the kid away. I thought, *Oh my God, how terrifying and horrifying that must be. What must the parents be dealing with if they are driven to do that to their own child?* I've really enjoyed giving Bree and Rex this bad kid to deal with. Shawn Pyfrom's this really good little teenage actor. So he's had a lot of fun with Andrew.

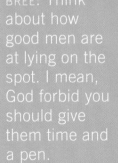

BREE: Think about how good men are at lying on the spot. I mean, God forbid you should give them time and a pen.

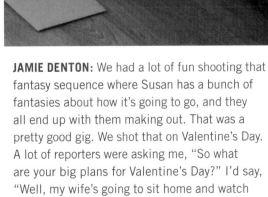

JAMIE DENTON: We had a lot of fun shooting that fantasy sequence where Susan has a bunch of fantasies about how it's going to go, and they all end up with them making out. That was a pretty good gig. We shot that on Valentine's Day. A lot of reporters were asking me, "So what are your big plans for Valentine's Day?" I'd say, "Well, my wife's going to sit home and watch *The Bachelorette* and I'm going to make out with Teri Hatcher. Happy Valentine's Day, honey!"

Episode

CHILDREN WILL LISTEN

117

On a visit to Andrew's boot camp, Bree and Rex learn that Andrew thinks he might be gay; Susan's mother, Sophie, comes for a visit; Paul tells Zach that a woman tried to steal him and that his parents couldn't let it happen; Lynette, unable to find a sitter, brings her kids to Bree's — and later learns that Bree has spanked Porter; Carlos, furious that Gabrielle kept the settlement secret, forces her to sign a postnuptial agreement; and Gabrielle conceives a child.

132

written by
KEVIN MURPHY

directed by
LARRY SHAW

LYNETTE: You're right, Bree. I've got a lot to learn about parenting. And I feel blessed to be getting sage advice from such an impeccable mother like you. I mean, your kids turned out perfect, as long as you don't count Andrew. Where is he again? Hm? Some kind of a boot camp for juvenile delinquents?

RICARDO ANTONIO CHAVIRA: I didn't realize that people were going to react so strongly to the plot about Carlos tampering with Gabrielle's birth control. I put the fear of God into women around the world. You hear stories about women who stop taking it and then the husbands get blindsided, so I think it's hilarious that it's reversing the perspective.

MARC CHERRY: With this pregnancy storyline we had a feeling some of the fans were ahead of us. She's having sex with two different guys and Carlos has been tampering with her birth control. So instead of doing a cliffhanger where she finds out she's pregnant in the last episode, we thought, *Let's reveal that she's pregnant earlier on, and then have other complications.* This episode was one of my favorite episodes of the season, the way these different people are dealing with their children. I love telling the audience at the beginning that she would be pregnant while she was making love to Carlos, and then at the end, we restate the pregnancy thing, and she's with John. No one is sure whose it is.

CARLOS
If there was
a chance I didn't have
to go to jail—

GABRIELLE
You had Laotian
convicts sewing casual
wear for two cents an
hour. Don't you think you
deserve a time out?

ZACH
I've never actually
been in Mrs. Huber's
house before.

FELICIA
Obviously you haven't
been missing much.
This is the place where
good taste goes to die.

LYNETTE
She could've tried
something else,
like a time out. Or she
could have simply
threatened
to spank 'em.

TOM
Yeah, 'cause that works
out so well when we do it.

GABRIELLE
Look, you really
want to get back at him?
Then kiss me.

JOHN
How's that going to help?

GABRIELLE
Because one day,
when the time is right,
I'm going to tell him
how he drove me right
into your arms.
And that's going to
kill him.

"LIFE IS A JOURNEY, ONE THAT IS MUCH BETTER TRAVELED
WITH A COMPANION BY OUR SIDE. BUT SOMETIMES
WE LOSE OUR COMPANIONS ALONG THE WAY AND THEN THE
JOURNEY BECOMES UNBEARABLE."

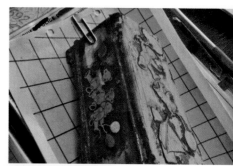

Episode

LIVE ALONE AND LIKE IT

118

Lynette grows closer to Mrs. McCluskey; Sophie tries to get Susan to go on a double date with her; Bree asks a minister to counsel Andrew away from being gay; and Gabrielle borrows John's credit card when finances at home get too tight. Mike gets the police file on Deirdre, and then sees Paul Young's name on the list of people who bought the baby chest.

134

written by
JENNA BANS

directed by
ARLENE SANFORD

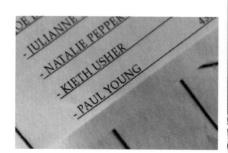

MARCIA CROSS: In the first part of the season there's a lot of jokey stuff with Bree, but in the second part she continues to deal with moralistic issues and gets put to the test. That has been more challenging than the first part of the season. For example, what it means to her that her son might be gay. She's begging him to get help because she actually believes if she doesn't save his soul he will go to hell. That's an honest-to–God emotionally painful place for her. That goes against my belief but *she* believes it's life or death.

GABRIELLE
If you ever hurt me
again I will kill you.

CARLOS
If you ever leave me for
another man I'll kill you.

GABRIELLE
Boy, with all this passion,
isn't it a shame that
we're not having sex?

SOPHIE
Tim is my guest
and he will go home
when I say so.

SUSAN
If he's not gone in
five minutes I'm going to
go out there and
tell him exactly how old
you really are.

JOHN
What other options do
you have—unless you
return the shoes and get
the money back?

GABRIELLE
Return the shoes? I can't
talk to you when you're
being hysterical!

REX
As far as I'm concerned,
if Andrew is happy
with who he is then it is
our job to support him.

BREE
Your father
is into S&M.

REX
Bree!

BREE
He makes me beat him
with a riding crop.
And I let him. It's no
wonder you're
perverted. Look who
your parents are.

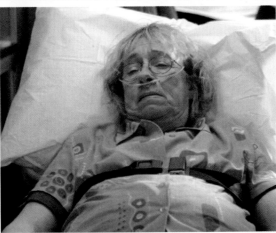

ANDREW: From now on, I'm going to be so good. I'm gonna eat my vegetables, I'm gonna get good grades, I'm gonna say "Yes, Ma'am" and "No, Ma'am." I'm gonna make her believe that God has delivered her this little miracle. Until one day, when she least expects it, I'm gonna do something so awful it is going to rock her world. I mean, it is really going to destroy her. And when that day comes, trust me, I'll know paradise.

BREE: Our son just told us that he might be gay. There are two hundred other boys in this camp. Now, I could explain to you what might happen if we left him here but I'm a lady and I don't use that kind of language.

FELICITY HUFFMAN: Kathryn Joosten is just wonderful. You expect from a little older actor—and she is only a little bit older—that they get tired more easily and they don't remember their lines as well. Once you're past 50, they say it just takes twice or three times as long. And Kathryn just blew all those expectations out of the water. She's saucy and would give me shit all the time and knew her lines backwards and forwards and would make a scene work beyond what was written. Most actors, deep down, want to be liked, so they'll soften the edges of a character, and Kathryn doesn't worry about being liked. Consequently, she is imminently adorable.

135

MARC CHERRY: A lot of the dialogue in the part where Bree has the Methodist preacher talk to Andrew was taken from my own experience when I came out to my mother. She made me go to a counseling session, and when I showed up, I found out it was Christian counseling. In that scene I show both sides, hers and his. She just wants him to understand where she's coming from but sadly, where she's coming from is a very hurtful place.

"SPRING COMES EVERY YEAR TO WISTERIA LANE. IT'S THE TIME WHEN
FLOWERS START TO BLOOM, WHEN BUTTERFLIES EMERGE
FROM THEIR COCOONS, WHEN BEES BEGIN TO SEARCH FOR NECTAR. SPRING
IS ALSO THE TIME WHEN A YOUNG MAN'S FANCY TURNS TO OBSESSION."

136

THERE IS NO WAY THE MAYER HOUSE WOULD BE WITHIN VIEW FROM THE ACTUAL SECTION OF WISTERIA LANE WHERE
SUSAN AND GABRIELLE ARE TALKING ABOUT GABRIELLE'S PREGNANCY (RIGHT BEFORE SUSAN'S HOUSE EXPLODES).

Zach continues to obsess over Julie; Lynette learns that
Tom is working with his ex-girlfriend, Annabel — and has kept
it secret; Gabrielle discovers she's pregnant; and Rex
becomes jealous of Bree's continuing friendship with George.
After Susan's tensions with Paul and Zach escalate, her
kitchen explodes and her house catches on fire. In a flashback
we learn that Mary Alice may have taken the baby son of a
troubled young woman she worked with.

written by
ADAM BARR

directed by
JEFF MELMAN

TERI HATCHER: The day we blew my house up, everyone and their sister came to Wisteria Lane. The number of people hanging around must have rivaled the day Oprah made her visit. When a house explodes, no one wants to miss the fireworks. Eva and I had a scene together in front of her house and then I was to look and see my kitchen was up in flames. After I realize it's my house, I panic and run down the street. To me, the nerve-wracking thing was, I was in high heels and a dress, and I knew after my house was set ablaze, I only had one chance to give the scene all I had. That means no tripping in heels. I made it down the street in one piece and in one take and was able to breathe a little easier after that.

137

ANNABEL: Yes, Tom and I were in love, but he married you. I'm not looking to break up a happy couple. Anyway, that's certainly more your speed, isn't it?

FELICITY HUFFMAN: I knew Melinda McGraw from a series we did ten or eleven years ago called *The Human Factor.* That was during a time in my life when I didn't know anyone in L.A. and she really befriended me and would take me hiking. She was always this really lovely, pretty person, an angel. Then I went back to New York and we lost touch. I didn't know she was playing Annabel until I walked in the makeup trailer and there she was. I was so pleased because that girl can act. One morning, Doug came into the makeup trailer and said hi to me and then quickly went down to the other end of the trailer where Melinda was getting her hair done. Suddenly he's sitting down at that end of the trailer a really long time. I said, "Let's run lines," and he's down there laughing and giggling. Before I know it, I say, "Stop flirting with Melinda and get over here and run lines with me!" That was a Lynette moment, and it helped me with the story.

MARC CHERRY: Originally, the plot was that Tom had a child with Annabel that he and Lynette didn't know about. The network just felt that was too much, that it would ruin the relationship for Lynette and Tom. It was very upsetting to Tom Spezialy and me because it was such a good secret. The complications were so rich.

"MARRIAGE IS A SIMPLE CONCEPT. BASICALLY,
IT'S A CONTRACT BETWEEN TWO PEOPLE THAT BINDS
THEM TOGETHER FOR LIFE IN THE HOPES
THAT THEY CAN LIVE HAPPILY EVER AFTER. SADLY,
SOME CONTRACTS ARE MADE TO BE BROKEN."

Episode

SUNDAY IN THE PARK WITH GEORGE

120

Morty and Sophie reunite; Lynette tries dressing up to win Tom's sexual attention; Edie witnesses Bree's budding "friendship" with George; Gabrielle tells John he might be the father of her baby; Susan learns from Kendra that Mike killed in self-defense; and after taking Zach in, Felicia convinces Paul to leave town.

written by
KATIE FORD

directed by
LARRY SHAW

FELICITY HUFFMAN: I've always felt bad around really pretty or really thin people. When you become a mother, it's at Mach Four level because you're always a mess. But I've always had a 40-year-old body and now that I'm 40, I feel like I look pretty good. When you're a mom you don't have time to take a shower, to work out, or get your hair done. What's so great about Melinda McGraw is that she is so sleek and beautiful with these enormous eyes and Lynette just says to herself, *I'm covered in jam.*

FELICIA: I'm sorry the copies are hard to read—I keep the originals in a safe place. Seemed like a reasonable precaution, since you murdered Martha and all. Would you like a cookie?

EVA LONGORIA: Every actor hates being pregnant on a show because you have to wear those awful fake stomachs and you end up getting the all the drab, crappy maternity clothes. So I asked Marc right from the get go, "Please don't make me pregnant!" And at the end of Season One I am pregnant. I asked him to wait until I got pregnant in real life so that we could write it in then. He said, "That's a good idea. When are you planning on getting pregnant?" I said, "In about five years," and he said, "Oh honey, you have to be pregnant before Season Five!"

MARC CHERRY: We wanted to do a whole comedic bit where Susan goes to Noah's house and they have peacocks, and she's waiting outside and gets attacked by a peacock. Then we found out that you can't train peacocks. But we did find some people who had geese. So we were going to have a bunch of geese attack Susan and then someone said, "Well, we only have six geese, and geese might be a little skittish." So our director came to us and said, "We only have a limited time in this location. Please write me something that's not geese." So we ended up with Susan being tackled by a security guard.

GABRIELLE
I feel a wave of morning sickness coming on and I want to be standing on your mother's grave when it hits.

MORTY
Don't give up on him. I mean, if I had given up, I wouldn't be here now with this lovely lady.

SUSAN
Did she tell you that he served time in prison for manslaughter?

MORTY
No. No, she left that part out.

LYNETTE
It soaked through a little. That is the nature of baby throw-up. You want me to wear a Hazmat suit or are you gonna be okay?

EDIE
You could have an affair with anyone and you choose a pharmacist? You are such a Republican.

Mike and Susan decide to move in together; Bree breaks
off her friendship with George and he tells her a lie to turn
her away from Rex; Carlos assaults Justin, thinking
he's Gabrielle's lover; Lynette's meddling makes Tom lose
out once again on a promotion; Mike kidnaps
Paul Young; and a new family moves to Wisteria Lane.

Episode

GOODBYE FOR NOW

124

written by
JOSH SENTER

directed by
DAVID GROSSMAN

FELICITY HUFFMAN: It was hard personally for me to do the scene where I go behind Tom's back and sabotage him. It wasn't premeditated. It happened in the moment. But still, it was hard to endorse the fact that I was selling my husband down the river. You have to endorse everything you're acting. Lynette's behavior has got to be something that is dealt with in the marriage. Otherwise, it's just going to be slow rot from the inside out.

140

EDIE
You said you two were finished. You thought he was a murderer.

SUSAN
And that was your cue to come over and flirt?! You wasted your time... and your donuts.

EDIE
Not if you choke on them.

JUSTIN
I'm gay.

CARLOS
This is not happening again.

SUSAN
I'll keep it warm for you.

MIKE
I'm afraid I'm gonna be too late for dinner.

SUSAN
I wasn't talking about dinner.

TERI HATCHER: Jamie Denton and his wife just had their baby and I thought, *What better time than now to throw them a baby shower?* Since our entire crew and production staff is quite large, I decided to throw it right in the middle of lunch on a Monday—in Susan's home. A few days before, I ordered my favorite cake for seventy. It ended up weighing over twenty pounds. I printed birth announcements that I wrapped over chocolate bars, burned a custom CD that was befitting a girl's party, and on the day of the big event, I brought in pink balloons, decorations, and a great Italian lunch for all to enjoy. It was a really special moment. Everyone came together to celebrate the birth of Malin. We felt like a family, all sitting side by side at long tables, enjoying the meal and time together.

EDIE: Oh, honey. You are so far out of your league that you're playing a whole different sport.

Episode

ONE WONDERFUL DAY

122

MARC CHERRY HAS KNOWN ACTOR DOUG SAVANT'S REAL-LIFE WIFE, LAURA LEIGHTON, SINCE 1985 WHEN LEIGHTON AND CHERRY WERE IN A PERFORMING GROUP CALLED "THE YOUNG AMERICANS."

142

Rex dies of a heart attack, after wondering if Bree poisoned him; Carlos goes to prison for gay bashing; Mike learns the truth from Paul about Deirdre's death — and lets him go free; Tom decides to be a stay-at-home dad and tells Lynette to go back to work; Zach holds Susan at gunpoint.

written by

**BY JOHN PARDEE
& JOEY MURPHY
AND MARC CHERRY
& TOM SPEZIALY
& KEVIN MURPHY**

directed by

LARRY SHAW

RICARDO ANTONIO CHAVIRA: In that scene where I lunge at Jesse's character people can see the full rage that is in my character. I'm yelling at him, "I'm gonna kill you, I'm gonna kill you." Then I broke into Spanish: *"Yo voy a matar!"* We shot the rehearsal the very first time and I just went for it. The director, Larry Shaw, came up to me and said, "Man, we should have had a camera facing the other way. The look on Jesse Metcalfe's face when you were coming at him—dude, he backed himself up against that wall." Then I looked, and Jesse had the most honest look of sheer terror. I think I scared the living shit out of him.

MARY ALICE: If you think I'm giving my baby to some junkie, you're crazy.

MARC CHERRY: The predicament of any working woman is that you can love your career, but there is something, there is something to be said for getting to stay home every day with your kids, and you don't want anyone else to be better at it than you are. My mom loved being home with us kids. It was important to her and to us. But at one point she had to work because my parents needed the money and we did not like her working. It's not a very feminist point of view, but for our family, it just really worked out that Mom was at home.

MARY ALICE
It's one of the unwritten rules of suburbia: don't call the neighbors in the middle of the night unless the news is bad.

GABRIELLE
We won't comfort. We're just gonna talk about noncrisis things.

SUSAN
Oh, I know! I found Mrs. Huber's journal in some of Mike's stuff. And I think she knew Mary Alice's secret and was blackmailing her.

LYNETTE
Yep. That'll do it.

CARLOS
Aren't we breastfeeding?

GABRIELLE
Oh honey, if you can swing that one, more power to you.

TOM
You tell me all the time how hard it is to be a mom.

LYNETTE
Well, yes. Yes, it is hard. But I love it, too. And I've been doing it for six years. And I haven't complained … the entire time.

143

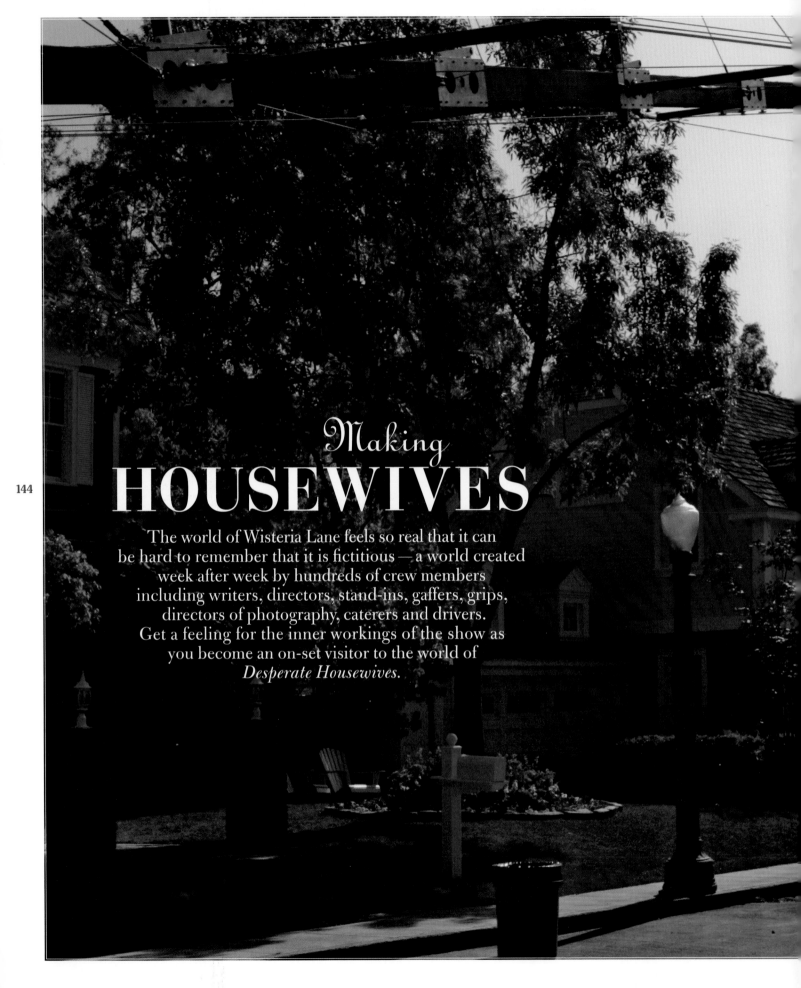

Making
HOUSEWIVES

The world of Wisteria Lane feels so real that it can
be hard to remember that it is fictitious — a world created
week after week by hundreds of crew members
including writers, directors, stand-ins, gaffers, grips,
directors of photography, caterers and drivers.
Get a feeling for the inner workings of the show as
you become an on-set visitor to the world of
Desperate Housewives.

THE TITLE SEQUENCE

In the beginning, there was a title sequence,
and a picture of Adam and Eve, and it was good.

As soon as the image of Adam and Eve comes on our television screens each Sunday night, we know *Housewives* is about to begin. The Santa Monica-based company that created the title sequence for the show, yU + Co., competed for the job with fifteen other production companies — and won the assignment on the basis of their creative vision.

Marc Cherry wanted the sequence to introduce desperate women from history, using classic paintings. Garson Yu, creative director of yU + Co., and his producer, Lane Jensen, began gathering research materials to show to the network: a Lucas Cranach the Elder painting of Adam and Eve, an Egyptian woman with her children, the Jan van Eyck portrait *The Marriage of Giovanni Arnolfini*

and Giovanna Cenami, and Grant Wood's *American Gothic*. He suggested the idea of connecting them with a pop-up book. The executives were excited enough to give them the job.

Once they got cracking, the production team selected their final images, finding out what they could license, and then created the virtual pop-up book. "Instead of linking the images with dissolves," says Yu, "we put all the images in this cardboard set, and we created a mechanical, robotic kind of movement, like in pop-up books."

Yu and his team had seen the pilot, which had already been shot, and tried to mimic the slightly heightened look of the show itself.

"Because the look of the show is very stylized, we wanted to create something stylized in our title sequence. The pop-up book brought the whole sequence to life and made it very nontraditional."

To match the comedic tone, they made sure that in each painting there was a vignette, a small joke. "Each joke represents a woman doing something desperate," Yu explains. "The apple falls from the tree on top of Adam, the Egyptian woman gets knocked over by her children, and the husband in the van Eyck tosses a banana peel that gets swept up by his wife. In *American Gothic*, the daughter watches her father go off with a younger woman

Although the title sequence has a wink-wink feel, Yu also wanted to insure that it maintained the slightly ominous mood of the pilot. "When you look at the image of Adam and Eve, and the image at the end, and the van Eyck, there is a subtle, dark tone to it. The snake is looking directly at the camera, representing temptation and seductiveness. And in the van Eyck the scene is reflected in the mirror behind them, which gives it the feeling of a mystery."

In the first pass at the title sequence, the actresses did not appear at all; the last frame was the Adam and Eve image from the beginning. The network

and then she gets put into a can of sardines. The woman in the 1950s image carrying the groceries drops them, and the can of soup, from the pop-art era, takes us into the Lichtenstein-like image of the woman punching her boyfriend. Then we come back to the Garden of Eden and introduce the characters' faces."

The Garden of Eden symbolism was intentional, Yu says. "You'll notice that the women are all holding an apple, which represents temptation, but they never bite into them because we want to keep the temptation open."

was not happy about this choice, Yu recalls. "They wanted to show the actors during the entire sequence but Marc was very insistent on not doing that. The compromise was to show them at the very end."

For the font, Yu's art director Yolanda Santosa selected a script font to give a more personal, handwritten feel. Once the images and order of the sequence was complete, composer Danny Elfman set it to music and Yu retooled the animatics to match the rhythm. "He is a really wonderful composer," says Yu. "His music always has this kind of playfulness to it, and a dark humor."

Whether you watch *Housewives* for the comedy, the drama, the mystery, or the realism, whatever draws you in comes from the hard work of Marc Cherry and his dedicated crew of writers. Ask any of the show's stars why the show is successful and they'll cite the writing, which is, after all, where everything begins.

WRITING HOUSEWIVES

Marc Cherry heads a staff of eleven writers, who bring a diverse set of backgrounds to the table. After the show was green-lit for its first season and the staff had been hired, Cherry guided them in figuring out where the season was going to go. On a whiteboard in the writers' room (which has since been transformed into a Ping-Pong room), the staff made a chart with the characters' names listed vertically and the

bors won't talk, and Edie learns by gossiping with Lynette that Susan is heartbroken over Mike.

Once a draft is in progress, the writers come up with a title for it that reflects its overall theme. Because Cherry is a huge Stephen Sondheim fan, almost all the shows in Season One are named after Sondheim songs—like "Goodbye for Now," "Every Day a Little Death," and "Children Will Listen."

episodes listed horizontally. Each character had a different color index card on which her stories would be written. As the writers filled in the stories, they extracted themes for each episode, like competition, children, or loneliness — themes that are articulated in Mary Alice's voiceovers.

"We'll come up with a couple of strong storylines," says Cherry, "and if a theme presents itself from those two, then we'll know to manipulate the next two stories to include it. Sometimes you have to get certain story beats done in an episode and very often you don't have to change much to be able to bring them into a given theme." For example, in the episode "The Ladies Who Lunch," all the stories deal with gossip: Bree learns that Maisy Gibbons had a black book, Lynette realizes someone has been saying her kids started a lice outbreak, Gabrielle hides her sewage problem so the neigh-

The Writers

MARC CHERRY

TOM SPEZIALY

KEVIN MURPHY

JOHN PARDEE

JOEY MURPHY

CHRIS BLACK

KATIE FORD

ADAM BARR

ALEXANDRA CUNNINGHAM

KEVIN ETTEN

JENNA BANS

JOSH SENTER

Certain writers tend to write for certain characters, based on their own life experience — Cherry, for example, writes for Bree, who is based on his mother; Kevin Murphy, a newlywed, writes for Tom and Lynette; Tom Spezialy, Tracey Stern, and Chris Black, all parents, often write parenting storylines. The writers' television background also informs how stories are assigned: John Pardee and Joey Murphy come from a sitcom background and write many of the more comedic scenes, and Alexandra Cunningham, who worked on *NYPD Blue,* writes the scenes between Mike and the police.

Though each episode is a collaborative process, only one or two writers are credited for each episode, according to what kind of deal each writer has. Cherry likes this way of working. "If there's a problem with a story, you need to have a draft in quickly so that you can see what's working and what isn't." At the beginning of Season One, Cherry was writing 80 to 100 percent of the episodes, but in the last episode, he says, "I have about three or four scenes in it. The writers have done a tremendous job of picking up my tonality and running with it."

Sometimes a writer will throw out a specific story from his or her life that will make its way onto the show. Early on in the season Cherry asked the writers the worst thing their mothers had done. His own mother had once left him and his siblings by the side of the road to punish them, so that was written. "She called me after the show," he jokes, "and was a little appalled."

Many plotlines are inspired by real-life news stories. The ADD-medication addiction came from a magazine article that Stern brought in about a suburban mother who had become addicted to her kids' medication, while the Maisy Gibbons storyline came from a real news story about an Orange County soccer mom who was turning tricks.

move on to the next thing. So I started getting into the next phase of their lives much more quickly than I anticipated."

For example, Cherry knew Susan and Mike would reunite at the end of Season One, but until they did he needed to give Susan other stories — so he came up with the idea of having her mother come to stay with her. The decision on whether to kill Martha Huber, a pivotal plot point, was hotly debated among the staff. "We debated for hours," says writer Kevin Murphy, "about whether to murder Martha Huber in Episode 107, whether it was right to kill her, and what it would cost the show. Ultimately it was an unexpected move to have Paul kill Martha, but it really helped the show, because it added this other element of the mystery that kept the scenes going, because of the murder investigation."

Frequently the writers create plot turns that are designed to mislead the audience as a way of keeping the story surprising. "We knew we wanted the audience to think there was a baby

Every writer gets rewritten, even Cherry. "Often I'll take a shot at a scene and it's not quite working," he says, "and I'll have something else to do. So I'll give it to a writer and say, 'Take a look at that. I think I need a joke there,' or 'I'm not happy with that ending.' There's no shame in being rewritten."

Because of the limited time available for each episode (they run about forty-two minutes each), many great scenes get shot but then wind up on the cutting-room floor. "The biggest problem we had in Season One," says Cherry, "is that we're so far behind in our schedule that these drafts come in really long and we don't have the time to cut them down to size."

As Season One took off, the writers found that many of the storylines needed to be advanced more quickly than they had intended. Recalls Cherry, "With a lot of my storylines I thought that I'd have eight or ten episodes to deal with an issue, and it turned out that after five or six I was ready to

inside the toy chest," says Murphy. "And the name Dana was also a red herring. Zach says, 'I killed my baby sister' when in fact his memory was faulty."

The key, of course, as the show continues, will be for the writers to come up with enough new plot turns and mysteries to keep audiences on the edge of their seats. "As we came down to the finish line for the first season," says Murphy, "the show got a little more dramatic, just because it was all about the mystery, so the comedy aspects of the show became a little smaller. As we move forward into Season Two the comedy will come back to the forefront, and we'll follow up on our new mysteries. And things will start to get bigger and more tense and scary as the season moves on."

THE MAP

With all the murder, mayhem and manipulation on
our favorite street, it can be hard to remember
who lives where on Wisteria Lane (which is actually
Universal Studios' Colonial Street).

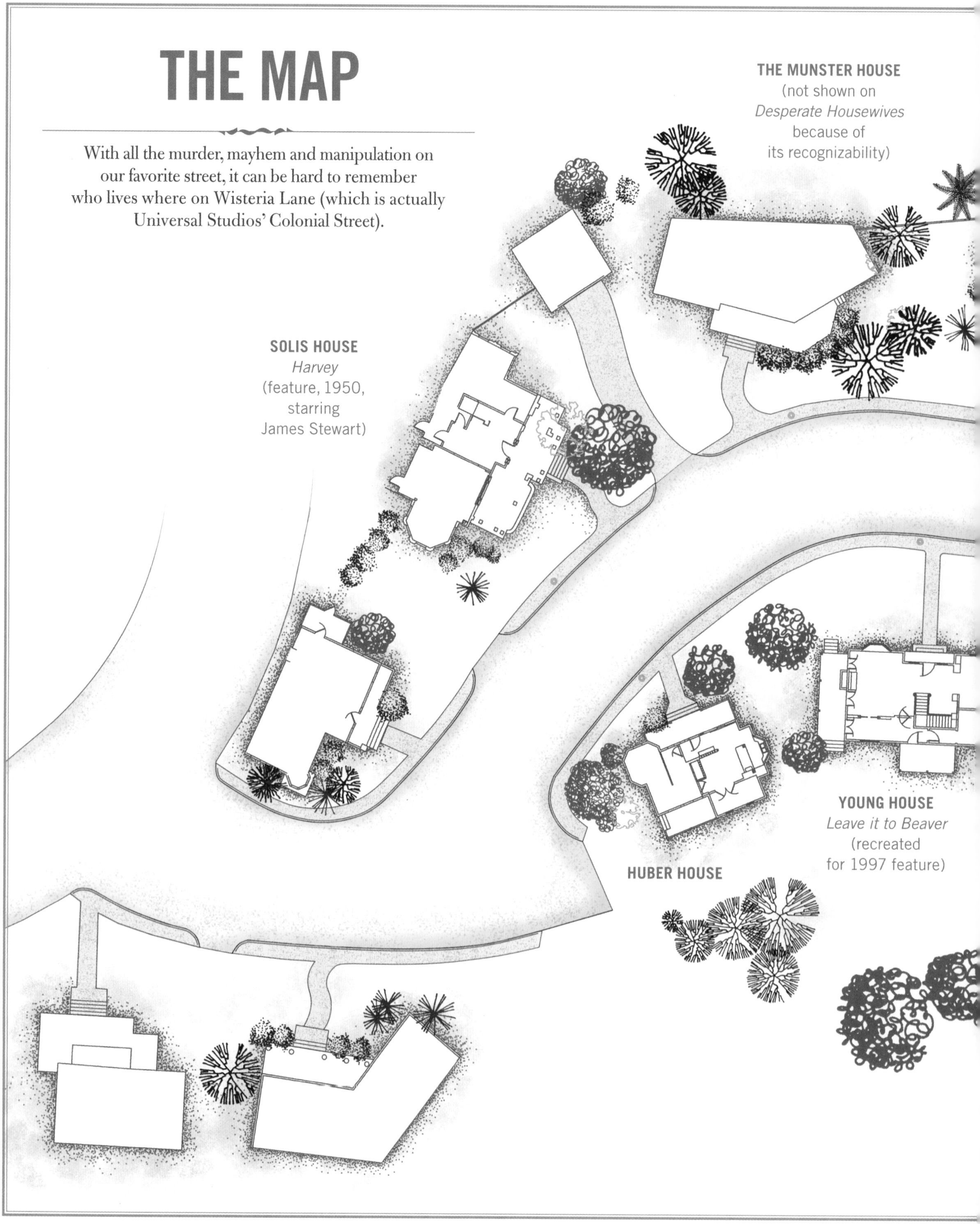

THE MUNSTER HOUSE
(not shown on
Desperate Housewives
because of
its recognizability)

SOLIS HOUSE
Harvey
(feature, 1950,
starring
James Stewart)

YOUNG HOUSE
Leave it to Beaver
(recreated
for 1997 feature)

HUBER HOUSE

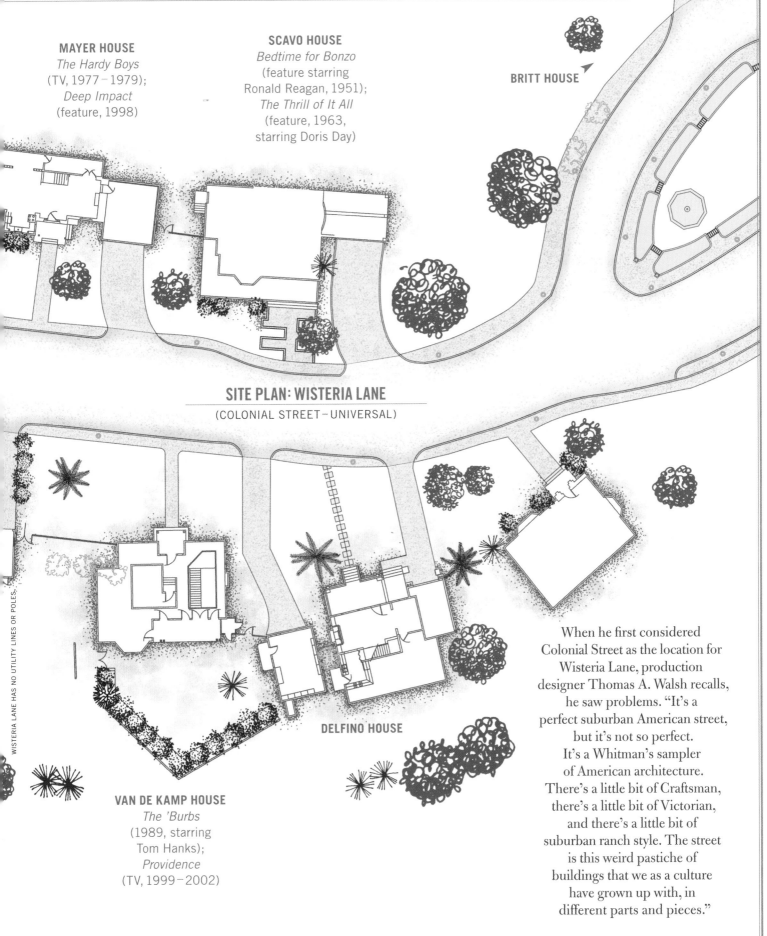

MAYER HOUSE
The Hardy Boys
(TV, 1977–1979);
Deep Impact
(feature, 1998)

SCAVO HOUSE
Bedtime for Bonzo
(feature starring
Ronald Reagan, 1951);
The Thrill of It All
(feature, 1963,
starring Doris Day)

BRITT HOUSE

SITE PLAN: WISTERIA LANE
(COLONIAL STREET – UNIVERSAL)

WISTERIA LANE HAS NO UTILITY LINES OR POLES.

VAN DE KAMP HOUSE
The 'Burbs
(1989, starring
Tom Hanks);
Providence
(TV, 1999–2002)

DELFINO HOUSE

When he first considered
Colonial Street as the location for
Wisteria Lane, production
designer Thomas A. Walsh recalls,
he saw problems. "It's a
perfect suburban American street,
but it's not so perfect.
It's a Whitman's sampler
of American architecture.
There's a little bit of Craftsman,
there's a little bit of Victorian,
and there's a little bit of
suburban ranch style. The street
is this weird pastiche of
buildings that we as a culture
have grown up with, in
different parts and pieces."

BUILDING HOUSEWIVES

When Marc Cherry hired Walsh to work on the show, the two began conceiving of the world of Wisteria Lane. They wanted the street — and the homes — to connote the Eisenhower era and traditional American values, but in a contemporary way. As part of his research, Walsh looked at advertising from the 1940s and 1950s and watched old TV shows like *Father Knows Best,*

The **SOLISES**
4349 WISTERIA LANE

The **MAYERS**
4353 WISTERIA LANE

Mrs. **HUBER**
4350 WISTERIA LANE

The **YOUNGS**
4352 WISTERIA LANE

As he began to plan his set design, Walsh wanted the different interiors to be clearly delineated because the show's editing style was so fast that audiences needed to know right away where they were. "You're constantly cutting between these four primary lives," says Walsh, "so in conceptualizing their environments we needed to come up with very strong

identities that represented those core characters, in terms of palette and style."

While all the environments suggest 1950s values, Walsh and his team work to insure that they look realistic and modern. "We don't want the look to be so far removed from real life that it becomes a style statement. Everyone needs to feel familiar with

My Three Sons, and *Leave it to Beaver,* whose exteriors were shot, coincidentally, on Universal's Colonial Street.

Walsh asked Cherry to write background on each of the characters to help him develop their environments. "I gave him a laundry list of characteristics," says Walsh, "like age, religion, occupation, and income on each of the characters and asked him to fill them in. Once we knew who these people were, all the departments — costume, locations, set — could think about how to reveal the differences between the characters."

The **SCAVOS**
4355 WISTERIA LANE

The **VAN DE KAMPS**
4354 WISTERIA LANE

MIKE DELFINO
4356 WISTERIA LANE

Wisteria Lane. It's easy to make it spooky, and go in that direction, but we're trying to avoid being too self-conscious. Our job is to support the script."

They also try to keep Wisteria Lane hovering somewhere between the real world and a fantasy world. For example, the license plates on all the cars say "The Eagle State," implying America. "But we don't know exactly where we are," says Walsh. "We know we're not in a red state or a blue state. I keep saying we're kind of in a pink state. We're somewhere in the middle of America's soul."

The Solises are the most conspicuous consumers, so Walsh created a "new money" home for them. "I think they're the only ones who had a decorator," he jokes, "and the decorator took advantage of them." He gave them religious paintings like the Madonna–and–child over the mantel to mock the fact that Gabrielle doesn't want children and to serve as a nod to the Solises' Catholicism. To contrast with the religious paintings, he also gave them Warhol-style portraits of Gabrielle on the stairway, and modeling pictures of her throughout the entryway. "Their world is all about narcissism, so we tried to have fun with it."

INSIDE
The SOLISES'

Gabrielle's Palette

DARK BEIGE
BEESWAX
ANNAPOLIS GRAY
SOFT PUMPKIN
ACORN YELLOW
SUMMER PEACH

Mary Alice's Palette

STRAW
GUILFORD GREEN
NANTUCKET GREY
PRINCETON GOLD
WARM TAN
TOWNSEND –
HARBOR BROWN

INSIDE
The YOUNGS'

The Young house interior is a composite of classic 1950s and 1960s television houses, from *Lassie* to *Father Knows Best*. Its exterior is the *Leave it to Beaver house*—fitting for a family in which everything seemed right on the outside. "We wanted a squeaky clean environment. The Youngs' secret was well-masked, so we designed in contrast to that, to make the house pleasant even though something scary had happened there."

Susan Mayer is artistic and eclectic in her style—so her home is shabby chic. "Susan is slightly scattered in terms of her focus and her passions," says Walsh, "so her environment is more whimsical. Her furnishings look like they were picked up at a flea market or yard sale." For example, the chairs at her dining room table don't match, there are a lot of small collectibles, and furniture from different eras."

The Scavos are the youngest family and have the most chaotic environment because of their many kids. "We went for the feeling that it's their first house together," says Walsh. "They bought an old house that was nicely remodeled. It has an open plan so we could reinforce the activity of kids running up and down the stairs. The furniture is new-looking, like it's from Restoration Hardware."

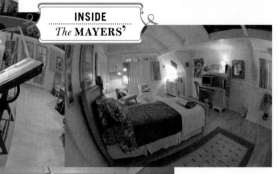

INSIDE
The MAYERS'

INSIDE
The SCAVOS'

Lynette's Palette

NOVEMBER SKIES
STRAWBERRY YOGURT
BEACON GRAY
CHERRY MALT
MELTED CREAM
ROSE SILK

Susan's Palette

PROVENCE CREME
WHISPER VIOLET
CRISP STRAW
HOLLINGSWORTH GREEN
SWEET SALMON
PINK PEARL

Bree's Palette

DURANGO DUST
WICKHAM GRAY
ARIZONA TAN
WYTHE BLUE
BUTTER PECAN
HATHAWAY PEACH

INSIDE
The VAN DE KAMPS'

The Van de Kamps are more old-money, upper-class WASPs—so the house has a staid, ordered look. "Because Bree and Rex's marriage has become stagnant in many ways," says Walsh, "we use a controlled palette, a lot of browns and beiges. It's lost its saturation." From any one room in the house you can see into two or three others, as a way of emphasizing mystery and secret, and remove.

SHOOTING HOUSEWIVES

WRITERS »   CASTING »

The process of shooting *Desperate Housewives* is complicated, intense, and fast. Though you only see eleven series regulars each week, over two hundred crewmembers are involved in putting each episode together. Though the show is a comedy, it is not shot like other conventional comedies, on a sound stage with an audience and multiple cameras, but with a single camera, like a film, which is much more time-consuming.

Executive producers Tom Spezialy and Michael Edelstein oversee every stage of the production process, making sure every scene goes smoothly and fixing any last-minute problems as they arise. "My job has both financial ramifications and creative ones, having to do with writing, shooting, and post-production," says Edelstein. "On every episode you're making thousands and thousands of choices. You have thousands and thousands of feet of film and you then decide what you want to assemble out of that."

Each episode has about a three-week production schedule: a week for preproduction, a week for production, and a week for post-production. The company shoots for about eight days, twelve to fourteen hours a day—an enormously grueling schedule for everyone, but necessary because each episode has about sixty scenes.

The first step of the production process is the writing, which begins months before the actors are asked to make themselves available. As soon as the writers finish their script outlines, "every department looks at the outlines," says Edelstein, "to see what kind of props and sets are needed and what locations we'll need. The casting department starts their work and the art department figures out what we are going to shoot on the lot and what we want to build."

Casting directors Junie Lowry-Johnson and Scott Genkinger, who have worked on *Six Feet Under* and *NYPD Blue*, are essential to hiring the many guest stars and day players that make the show memorable. As the show has gotten more popular, they have had to field more requests from actors to do guest spots on the show—like Marlee Matlin, whose role was written specifically for her. Some special guest stars like Lesley Ann Warren and Bob Newhart are offered their roles without having to read for them.

SETS »

Production designer Thomas A. Walsh supervises all of the set decisions. "The art department is an umbrella for set dressing, props, and locations," he explains. Most of the home interiors are shot on the Universal City lot but when special locations are required—such as the Saddle Ranch Chop House, George's pharmacy, or the backyard for Carlos' going away party, the company goes on location. Two location scouts, David Foster and Rod Bacote, scout locations once they get the script outline, and then they take photos and bring them back to the director and producers. The mall where Gabrielle models the Buick was Sherman Oaks Fashion Square, for example, and the pharmacy is in Toluca Lake, a short drive from Universal City.

For sets like a doctor's office or principal's office, there is a set on the lot that can be adjusted as the script requires. The same set has been used for the principal's office, the juvenile rehabilitation center, and hospital rooms, while another was used for Maisy's bedroom and Dr. Goldfine's office. For the pilot scene where we catch a glimpse of Lynette in the boardroom, says Edelstein, "All that was there was a wall and a table. If you know what the camera's going to do, you just build appropriately for that, because every wall costs money."

COSTUME »

The costume department, headed by Catherine Adair, works from the episode outlines to prepare for the specific needs of the episode. If there's a specialty item, like Lynette's black dress in the pilot, which she wears into the pool, or Susan's fashion show dress which gets torn, the department needs extra time to create multiple copies for multiple takes.

MAKE-UP »

Makeup and hair are essential on a show featuring five strong female leads. The actors begin their day in the makeup trailer, which also serves as a place for them to chat, listen to music, and run lines. "First and foremost," says Edelstein, "hair and makeup serves the characters. The Bree flip is essential to Bree's character." Once the actors have their hair done, hair crewmembers are assigned to go to set and touch them up between takes, insuring that Bree's hair looks perfectly set and Susan's never does. "Teri can be incredibly glamorous," says Edelstein, "and I think it's to her credit that she always wants to appear real and natural. She is a gorgeous woman with incredible features but she goes to great lengths to insure that she looks like a mom."

Because hair is so easily affected by wind and weather changes, much of the crew's job is to provide continuity from take to take. They take endless Polaroids throughout the day to make sure that shots match. "It can take seven or eight hours to shoot one scene," says Edelstein, "Over the course of seven or eight hours, if the hair suddenly falls differently, when you cut the film together you have a disaster on your hands." Script supervisor Brenda Weisman corrects actors if they are saying their lines incorrectly so that each episode flows together properly.

The props department is responsible for any material item that is handled by an actor—a note is a prop, but a lamp is part of the set. If a lamp gets smashed over someone's head, it's a prop. Certain props take extra time to be constructed, like the popsicle-stick Trojan horse Julie makes in the pilot.

The most important production member for each episode is the director, who supervises all aspects of production on a given episode. In the first season *Housewives* has used a solid company of regular directors, including Larry Shaw, Jeff Melman, David Grossman, and Arlene Sanford. At any given time, three directors will be working—one on prep, one on production, and one on post. Because of the show's quirky sensibility, the producers demand a lot of the directors. "Some directors are used to very straight-ahead storytelling," says Cherry. "In our show, I depend upon the director to bring a lot to the party with visual humor. And it can be very difficult."

Once the cast arrives on set for a given scene, the director walks them through the blocking, or physical choreography of the moment. "The rehearsals are as much for the director and the crew as anyone else," Edelstein explains. "It's less about performance and more about where to put the cameras, how many shots you're going to need, and what needs to get accomplished."

Because the writers often rewrite scripts up until the last minute, many actors get script changes a day before they have to shoot the scene. "There's a lot of responsibility and a lot of challenge for the actors," says Edelstein. "If you get six pages of dialogue to memorize at eleven o'clock at night, you have to be at work at six-thirty in the morning, that's not easy."

There are two DPs, or directors of photography, who shoot the episodes: Walt Fraser and Lowell Peterson. One preps with the director while the other shoots. Each episode is shot on 35-millimeter, three-perforation film, which gives the film stock the rich look for which the show is known.

The director works with the DP to determine which takes were best, opting to print only some of the takes that are shot over the course of a day, because printing film is so expensive. Sometimes they print two takes, other times as many as six or twelve. The nonprinted scenes, referred to as B-neg, are kept in case a given print doesn't look good, so the director can go back and print it during post-production if necessary.

EXECUTIVE PRODUCER MICHAEL EDELSTEIN, ACTOR JAMES DENTON, PRODUCTION DESIGNER THOMAS A. WALSH, LINE PRODUCER GEORGE PERKINS, AND UNIT PRODUCTION MANAGER CHARLES SKOURAS ALL WORKED TOGETHER ON THE ABC SHOW *THREAT MATRIX* BEFORE COLLABORATING AGAIN ON *HOUSEWIVES*.

Each day's shots are processed and sent to the editors and key production members so everyone can see them. "It lets you know where you stand," says Edelstein, "and lets you know if anything is particularly wrong with the film, the light, or the performances." Immediately the editors, Jonathan Posell, Troy Takaki, and Andy Doerfer, begin assembling the scenes as they get them, putting together the best version of a scene. They use what's called temp, or temporary music, to score the scene—usually music that's been used on the show before.

Once in a while the producers decide a scene isn't working, and when this happens, they must reshoot, rescheduling the actors to come back and do the scene again. In Episode 101, where Edie and Mrs. Huber are in the remains of Edie's house, the scene was originally written with the two women and an insurance adjuster. Walsh had built a burned-out house on the sound stage but the consensus was that it looked fake, so instead the crew built a house out on the street, looking onto Wisteria Lane, and the scene was shot there. "When we reshot we cut the insurance adjuster out," says Cherry. "The episode had comein long and we needed a shorter scene, so since we were re-shooting it, we took the guy out so there were fewer lines. It was a much better scene because it was quicker, the visual was stronger, and you could see the actual street. The studio has been amazing about reshoots. They probably aren't going to be so generous in the second season because reshoots are so expensive."

A day or two later after the editors make their cut, the director creates a director's cut, which gets sent to the producers for their feedback. These cuts are often seven or eight minutes too long, and the producers work with the director to pare them down to the essential moments. This is why some scenes, like Edie in a motel room with Mr. Shaw, often get cut in postproduction. Each episode must be no longer than 42 minutes long to fit into an hour's worth of television time.

Once a cut is locked, the composer, Steve Jablonsky, along with the producers, "spot" where they want the music before he composes it. "Music is a really interesting element in our show," says Edelstein. "Because we are a quirky show, and we're not a traditional drama or a traditional comedy, the music has to walk a fine line. Sometimes we'll score a dramatic scene with fun music just to give it an edge, and sometimes we take a really funny scene and score it with dramatic music to make it funnier. Music guides the audience emotionally on how to react."

After the producers sign off on a cut, the studio, Touchstone Television, looks at it, and then ABC takes the final look. Occasionally scenes must be altered, either because they are deemed too lewd or simply because they're not working well. "It's all a process," says Edelstein. "Everything is in flux and people weigh in at different times. Sometimes we say they're absolutely right, and sometimes we say, 'You know what? We think it's great the way it is.'"

Edelstein says the show's seriocomic style makes it more challenging than a traditional drama might be. "Making comedy is harder than making drama. Mediocre drama plays okay but mediocre comedy just lands there and stinks. There's just no middle ground with comedy."

Desperate Housewives

BY MARC CHERRY

Though the nation caught its first glimpse of the show on October 3, 2004, the process of creating the show began years earlier, when Cherry dreamed up the idea of a show about desperate housewives while watching the Andrea Yates trial on television with his mother. His original pilot script, written in the summer of 2002, was much longer than the final shooting script, and contained different character names, many scenes that were never shot, and moments unseen by viewers. This version of the show's pilot got Marc Cherry his new agents at Paradigm, who loved it but told him, "You've got to emphasize the soap opera element." They put him in touch with *Housewives* co-executive producer Charles Pratt, who loved the script and encouraged Cherry to further emphasize the mystery storylines—by making Mike have a secret as well as Mary Alice, and heightening the drama within the Young family. He did, and his subsequent draft sold to ABC. The rest is *Housewives* history.

First Draft

AUGUST 15, 2002

FADE IN:

EXT. SUBURBAN STREET - DAY

We're driving down a tree-lined
suburban street. We finally stop at
a well-kept UPPER MIDDLE-CLASS house
complete with white picket fence.

MARY ALICE (V.O.)
My name is Mary Alice Scott.
When you read this morning's paper
you may come across an article about
the unusual day I had last week.

CLOSE-UP - MARY ALICE SCOTT

The camera pulls back to reveal an
ATTRACTIVE WOMAN IN HER EARLY 30'S
wearing gardening gloves emerging from
the house. She crosses to the flower
bed and begins pruning.

MARY ALICE (V.O.)
Normally there's never anything
newsworthy about my life. But that
all changed last Thursday.

INT. SCOTT HOUSE - KITCHEN - DAY

Mary Alice's HUSBAND AND SON are seated
at a table. She is busy serving them
BREAKFAST.

MARY ALICE (V.O.)
Of course, everything seemed quite
normal at first.

INT. SCOTT HOUSE - LAUNDRY ROOM - DAY

Mary Alice puts some clothes into the
WASHING MACHINE.

MARY ALICE (V.O.)
I performed my chores.

EXT. DRY CLEANERS - DAY

Mary Alice emerges from a dry cleaners
with some CLOTHING encased in PLASTIC.

MARY ALICE (V.O.)
I ran my errands.

EXT. SCOTT HOUSE - BACKYARD - DAY

Mary Alice paints some LAWN FURNITURE.

MARY ALICE (V.O.)
I completed my projects.

INT. SCOTT HOUSE - KITCHEN - DAY

Mary Alice goes around ADJUSTING
little BRIC-A-BRAC around the room.

MARY ALICE (V.O.)
In truth, I spent the day as I spent
every other day. Quietly polishing
the routine of my life until it
gleamed with perfection.

INT. SCOTT HOUSE - LIVING ROOM - DAY

Mary Alice is in the middle of the
IMMACULATE room. She is STANDING
completely STILL. As if FROZEN.

MARY ALICE (V.O.)
Which is why it was so astounding
when late last Thursday afternoon
...

INT. SCOTT HOUSE - HALLWAY - DAY

Mary Alice stands on a chair and
reaches up to the top shelf of the hall
closet. She brings down a REVOLVER.

MARY ALICE (V.O.)
... I decided to take a loaded gun
from the hallway closet and empty
its contents into my head.

CLOSE on A GUN FIRING.

MARY ALICE falls to the floor.

We see what appears to be BLOOD
spreading out over some tile. Suddenly
a woman's HAND wipes it away.

INT. HUBER HOUSE - KITCHEN - CONTINUOUS

We're in the kitchen of EDITH HUBER, a
plump woman in her late 40's, who has
just spilled some TOMATO SAUCE onto her
kitchen counter. She is wiping it up
when she suddenly HEARS something from
outside.

MARY ALICE (V.O.)
My body was discovered by my next-
door neighbor, Mrs. Edith Huber, who
had been startled by what she would
later describe to the police as a
strange popping sound.

EXT. HUBER HOUSE - BACKYARD - DAY

Edith crosses to the FENCE and JUMPS
up several times trying to PEER OVER.

BRENDA STRONG: Before I came in I read the pilot and saw the one they had shot with Sheryl Lee as Mary Alice. That was really helpful, but I could see what I had to offer in that role that, was different than what was done in the original. It's a little strange when you watch someone else in a role you're auditioning for because his or her performance lives in your mind. It can be hard to try to distinguish yourself sometimes, but I had fun with it.

161

2

Seeing nothing, she goes back inside her home.

> MARY ALICE (V.O.)
> Her curiosity aroused, Mrs. Huber quickly tried to think of a reason for dropping in on me unannounced.

INT. HUBER HOUSE - KITCHEN - DAY

Edith crosses to her kitchen pantry. She reaches inside and pulls out a BLENDER that has a tag on the side.

CLOSE ON TAG THAT READS 'PROPERTY OF MARY ALICE SCOTT.'

> MARY ALICE (V.O.)
> After some initial hesitation, she decided to return the blender she had borrowed from me six months before.

EXT. HUBER HOUSE - FRONT YARD - DAY

Edith exits her front door, CARRYING THE BLENDER, and crosses to Mary Alice's front door. She KNOCKS. She waits for a response. Nothing.

She goes to the side of the house and peers in the window. She suddenly sees Mary Alice's lifeless BODY. She SCREAMS.

INT. HUBER HOUSE - KITCHEN - CONTINUOUS

Edith runs in, puts the BLENDER on the counter and quickly picks up the PHONE.

> MRS. HUBER
> (emotional)
> Hello?! You've got to send an ambulance! It's my neighbor - omigod - there's blood everywhere! Yes! I think she's been shot! Please. You've got to send someone now!

Edith hands up the PHONE. She stands there for a beat, TEARY-EYED.

> MARY ALICE (V.O.)
> And for a moment, Mrs. Huber wept in her kitchen, overcome by this senseless tragedy. But only for a moment. If there was one thing Mrs. Huber was known for, it was her ability to look on the bright side.

Edith reaches down to the blender and RIPS the tag reading 'PROPERTY OF MARY ALICE SCOTT' off. She then puts the BLENDER back into HER pantry.

SMASH CUT TO:

MAIN TITLES

FADE IN:

EXT. SCOTT HOUSE - FRONT YARD - DAY

A SUNNY afternoon. Various people are walking up to the house, dressed in BLACK and carrying COVERED DISHES.

> MARY ALICE (V.O.)
> I was laid to rest on a Monday afternoon. After the funeral, all the residents of Wisteria Lane descended upon my home to pay their respects. And, as people do in these situations, they brought food.

EXT. SCOTT HOUSE - SIDEWALK - DAY

CLOSE ON LYNETTE SCAVO.

We pull back to reveal a worn-down LYNETTE carrying a CASSEROLE DISH.

> MARY ALICE (V.O.)
> Lynette Scavo, who lives down the block, brought fried chicken. Lynette had a great family recipe for fried chicken.

INT. COLLEGE LIBRARY - NIGHT

A SERIOUS twenty-year-old Lynette is intently reading a book.

> MARY ALICE (V.O.)
> Of course, she didn't have the time to make it while she was at Harvard.

INT. OFFICE - DAY

A CONFIDENT twenty-four-year-old Lynette is giving a presentation to a group of EXECUTIVES.

> MARY ALICE (V.O.)
> She certainly didn't have the time when she started working in advertising ...

MARC CHERRY: We changed Mary Alice Scott to Mary Alice Young because we couldn't get the name cleared with our lawyers. If over three people in the country have that name you're fine but with anything less than that, they make you use a different name. Apparently there was one Mary Alice Scott in the country.

MC: I had the line about Lynette going to Harvard because originally we had three flashbacks for every character but I changed it to two. My original draft was pretty long so I was looking for cuts anywhere I could get them.

INT. OFFICE - DAY

A PROUD thirty-year-old Lynette is posing for a PHOTO. Behind her is a door that reads LYNETTE SCAVO, VICE-PRESIDENT.

> MARY ALICE (V.O.)
> ... or while she was moving up the corporate ladder.

INT. DOCTOR'S OFFICE - DAY

Lynette and her husband, TOM, are staring in SURPRISE as a doctor points to images on an ULTRA-SOUND machine.

> MARY ALICE (V.O.)
> But when her doctor announced Lynette was pregnant with twins, her husband, Tom, had an idea.

CLOSE ON LYNETTE'S HUSBAND MOUTHING THE FOLLOWING WORDS:

> MARY ALICE (V.O.)
> "Why not just quit your job? It'll be better for our kids. And you'll love being a stay-at-home mom. It'll be so much more relaxing for you."

LYNETTE considers this for a moment, then weakly SMILES and nods in agreement.

INT. SCOTT HOUSE - FRONT YARD - DAY

We cut back to the earlier images of a worn-down LYNETTE carrying a CASSEROLE DISH.

> MARY ALICE (V.O.)
> But this was not the case. In fact, Lynette's life was so hectic ...

We pull back even farther to reveal LYNETTE is also pushing a stroller with PATSY, her one-year-old TODDLER. Her six-year-old TWIN sons, PETER and PAUL, and their five-year-old brother, PRESTON, are walking on the sidewalk in front of her.

> MARY ALICE (V.O.)
> ... she was now forced to get her fried chicken from a fast-food restaurant.

Suddenly Lynette's TWINS start ELBOWING each other as they walk down the sidewalk. Lynette looks at them WEARILY.

> MARY ALICE (V.O.)
> Lynette would've appreciated the irony of the situation, if she ever stopped to think about it. But she couldn't. She didn't have the time.

> LYNETTE
> (angrily)
> Boys, knock it off.

Suddenly one of the boys pushes another, sending him into the third. All three boys start BRAWLING.

> LYNETTE
> (screaming)
> DID YOU HEAR ME? I SAID KNOCK IT OFF!

She pushes the STROLLER to the side and then rushes over and SEPARATES her FIGHTING children.

> LYNETTE
> I mean it! When we go in there, you are going to behave yourselves.

> PAUL
> But he was the one who ...

> LYNETTE
> No buts! You're not gonna humiliate me in front of the entire neighborhood. And just so you know how serious I am about this ...

Lynette reaches into her pocket and pulls out a SLIP of PAPER. She holds it up in front of the boys.

> PETER
> What's that?

> LYNETTE
> This is Santa's cell phone number.

> PAUL
> (suspicious)
> How did you get that?

> LYNETTE
> I know somebody who knows somebody who knows an elf. Now, if any of you acts up, so help me, I'll call Santa and tell him. And then you'll be lucky if you get dirt for Christmas. Got it?

The boys NOD their heads nervously.

MC: I thought it was an interesting stylistic device to have the characters mouthing Mary Alice's voiceover. I was trying to throw in as many stylistic things as I could to make it different but that takes a little too long. Now, since we have less of it, you don't need the device as much.

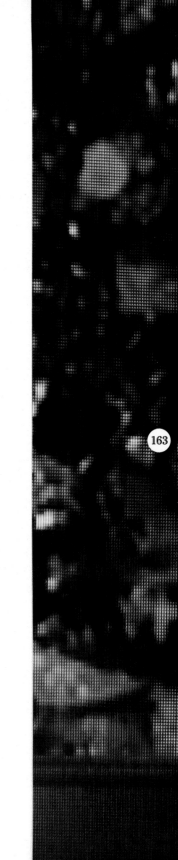

MC: My former roommate and best friend for years is Dan Solis. We met when I was in my twenties and he was my roommate for eight years. One day he mentioned to me something about being Mexican, and I looked at him and said, "Oh you are?" I had never thought about it. And in that moment it occurred to me that if someone's the same as you culturally and economically, it becomes very easy to overlook race. Dan is so happy that I put the name on the show because now people are starting to know how to pronounce his name.

MC: We couldn't use the line about her relationship being chilly like the gazpacho because the Solis house has one of the smaller front door-to-sidewalk ratios, so there wasn't enough walking going on for the whole voiceover. I had originally envisioned a longer walkway.

LYNETTE
Good. Now let's get this over with.

As Lynette stands up, MRS. HUBER suddenly crosses by.

MRS. HUBER
Hello, Lynette. I see you've brought the children.

LYNETTE
My baby-sitter won't return my phone calls. Get off my back.

Lynette BREEZES past Mrs. Huber towards the front door.

EXT. SOLIS - FRONT YARD - DAY

We see GABRIELLE SOLIS, a glamorous woman in her late 30's, emerge from the front door carrying a large TUPPERWARE bowl.

MARY ALICE (V.O.)
Gabrielle Solis, who lives two doors down, brought chilled gazpacho.

CLOSE ON GABRIELLE STRUTTING DOWN HER FRONT WALK.

INT. MANHATTAN FASHION SHOW

CLOSE ON GABRIELLE STRUTTING DOWN A RUNWAY.

MARY ALICE (V.O.)
Since her modeling days in New York, Gabrielle had always had a thing for Spanish cuisine and Spanish men.

As Gabrielle PASSES by we push in on CARLOS, who is seated in the audience. He is WATCHING Gabrielle intently.

INT. MANHATTAN RESTAURANT - NIGHT

Gabrielle and Carlos are SEATED in an ELEGANT restaurant.

MARY ALICE (V.O.)
It had been just two years since Carlos proposed.

Carlos suddenly takes a VELVET BOX out of his pocket and puts it on the table. Gabrielle is STUNNED.

MARY ALICE (V.O.)
Carlos, who specialized in mergers and acquisitions, was direct and to-the-point.

CLOSE ON CARLOS MOUTHING THE FOLLOWING WORDS:

MARY ALICE (V.O.)
I'm rich and you're beautiful. What do you say we get married and lead the kind of life that'll make all our friends jealous?

Carlos SMILES. Gabrielle LAUGHS, then THINKS for a moment.

MARY ALICE (V.O.)
Gabrielle, who had been looking to get off the runway before she was pushed off, said yes.

CLOSE ON CARLOS'S FACE. TEARS WELL UP IN HIS EYES.

MARY ALICE (V.O.)
She was touched when tears welled up in Carlos's eyes. But she soon discovered this happened every time Carlos closed a big deal.

EXT. SOLIS HOUSE - FRONT YARD - DAY

We cut back to GABRIELLE strutting down her front walk. She joins CARLOS who has obviously been WAITING for her.

MARY ALICE (V.O.)
So Gabrielle now had everything she'd always wanted. A big house, lots of credit cards and a housekeeper who made her chilled gazpacho anytime she wanted.

Gabrielle SHOVES the gazpacho into Carlos's hands.

MARY ALICE (V.O.)
But the gazpacho was not quite as chilled as Gabrielle's current relationship with her husband.

Gabrielle starts to cross the STREET. Carlos follows her.

CARLOS
Hey, if you talk to Al Mason at this thing I want you to casually mention how much I paid for your necklace.

GABRIELLE
(annoyed)
Oh, for God's sake ...

CARLOS
Hey, he let me know how much he paid
for his wife's new Jag. Just work it
into the conversation.

GABRIELLE
And how am I supposed to do that?

CARLOS
I'm sure you can think of a way.

GABRIELLE
I can't do it.

CARLOS
At the Donahues' party, everyone
was talking about mutual funds
and you found a way to mention you
once screwed Jon Bon Jovi *and* his
brother.

GABRIELLE
You know, Carlos, there is a
difference between bragging and
entertaining cocktail conversation.

Gabrielle SWEEPS past Carlos up the
walk to the SCOTT HOUSE and KNOCKS on
the front door.

INT. SCOTT HOUSE - LIVING ROOM - DAY

CLOSE ON A HAND REACHING FOR A DOOR
KNOB.

The door swings open to reveal two
GIFT BASKETS. We pull back to see
that they are carried by BREE VAN DE
KAMP. BEAUTIFUL and immaculately PUT-
TOGETHER, she enters with a confident
air.

MARY ALICE (V.O.)
Bree Van de Kamp, who lives on the
corner, brought baskets of muffins
and cookies she baked from scratch.
Bree was known for her baking.

INT. VAN DE KAMP HOUSE - SEWING ROOM
- DAY

Bree is at a SEWING machine.

MARY ALICE (V.O.)
And for making her own clothes.

EXT. VAN DE KAMP HOUSE - BACK YARD - DAY

Bree is RAKING a vegetable garden with
a HOE.
MARY ALICE (V.O.)
And for her gardening.

INT. VAN DE KAMP HOUSE - LIVING ROOM
- DAY

Bree puts two FABRIC SWATCHES on the
couch.

MARY ALICE (V.O.)
And for her interior decorating.

INT. SCOTT HOUSE - LIVING ROOM - DAY

We go back to the same shot of BREE at
the door holding her two GIFT BASKETS.
She SMILES and chats for a few seconds
with the people near the doorway. She
then BREEZES into the party.

MARY ALICE (V.O.)
Yes, Bree's many talents were known
throughout the neighborhood. And
everyone on Wisteria Lane thought of
Bree as the perfect wife and mother.
(then)
Everyone, that is, except her
family.

REX VAN DE KAMP, 40, ANDREW VAN DE
KAMP, 15, and DANIELLE VAN DE KAMP,
13, suddenly appear in the door frame.
They all wear a WEARY expression. They
follow Bree into the wake.

We cut to PAUL SCOTT, a middle-aged man
who is SOMBERLY greeting guests. BREE
walks DIRECTLY up to him.

BREE
(gravely)
Paul.

MR. SCOTT
Hello, Bree.
(off baskets)
Wow. You shouldn't have gone to all
this trouble.

BREE
No trouble at all. Now the red
basket is filled with desserts for
your guests. But the blue basket is
just for you and the kids. It's got
rolls and muffins. Breakfast-type
things.

MR. SCOTT
Thank you.

MC: The Disney lawyers wouldn't let me use the Jon Bon Jovi line, which killed me. They said he might be insulted and might sue. I was thinking, *I don't know of any man that would be insulted if Eva Longoria said she slept with them.* We could say the Yankees instead because it's an entire team and you're not specifying any particular individuals.

MC: When we were sending the script out I wanted the kids to come off younger because I didn't want to frighten actresses that they would have a 17-year-old son. So I downed those ages a little bit. Fortunately Marcia Cross wouldn't care. I could give her a 24-year-old son and she wouldn't care. But that was a calculated decision sending out the script. I was also concerned that studios and networks wouldn't want a show with female characters over 40, which is ironic given that our entire cast is over 40 except for little Eva.

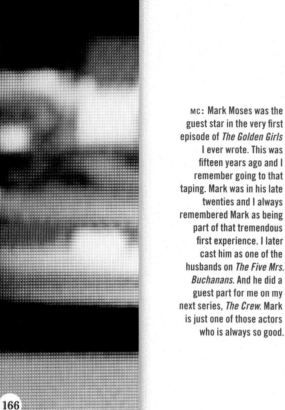

6

BREE
The least I could do was make sure you had a decent meal to look forward to in the morning. I know you're just out of your mind with grief.

MR. SCOTT
Yes, I am.

BREE
Of course, I will need the baskets back once you're done.

Bree CROSSES away. Mr. Scott looks over at Bree's family who all SHAKE their heads in mortification.

INT. CAR - DAY

CLOSE ON SUSAN MEYER

We pull back to reveal SUSAN is PARKING her car in front of the SCOTT HOUSE. On the dashboard is a CASSEROLE DISH that is covered with tin foil. SUSAN, who is normally FUN AND GOOD-NATURED, is in a contemplative mood.

MARY ALICE (V.O.)
Susan Meyer, who lives across the street, brought macaroni and cheese. Her husband, Karl, always teased her about her macaroni saying it was the only thing she knew how to cook and she rarely made it well.

INT. MEYER HOUSE - KITCHEN - EVENING

CLOSE ON TWO HANDS PICKING UP A CASSEROLE DISH.

We pull back to see a BEAMING SUSAN is taking the dish and SETTING it on a TABLE. Seated at the table are her husband, KARL, and a TWO-MONTH OLD JENNA in a high chair. Moving boxes are in the background.

MARY ALICE (V.O.)
It was too salty the night she and Karl moved into their house.

INT. MEYER HOUSE - KITCHEN - EVENING

CLOSE ON TWO HANDS PICKING UP A CASSEROLE DISH.

We pull back to see TEARY-EYED SUSAN is taking the dish and slamming it down on the table. Seated at the table is a FOUR-YEAR-OLD JENNA in a high chair.

MARY ALICE (V.O.)
It was too watery the night she smelled perfume on Karl's shirt.

Susan picks up a DRESS SHIRT slung over one of the chairs. She stares at it then THROWS it on the FLOOR.

INT. MEYER HOUSE - KITCHEN - EVENING

CLOSE ON ONE HAND PICKING UP A CASSEROLE DISH.

We pull back to see an ENRAGED SUSAN is taking the dish and placing it quietly on the table with one hand and is eavesdropping on the PHONE with the other. An EIGHT-YEAR-OLD JENNA is seated at the table.

MARY ALICE (V.O.)
She burned it the night she overheard Karl on the phone with his secretary.

Susan suddenly SMASHES the phone against the KITCHEN WALL.

EXT. SCOTT FRONT YARD - DAY

SUSAN gets out of her car with the MACARONI AND CHEESE. She is joined on the sidewalk by a TEN-YEAR-OLD JENNA. They start walking toward the SCOTT house.

MARY ALICE (V.O.)
It had been two years since Susan had divorced Karl. And though she was content, she had started to think how nice it would be to have a man in her life who'd make fun of her cooking.

JENNA looks over at SUSAN.

JENNA
Mom, can I ask you something?

SUSAN
Sure, sweetie.

JENNA
Why did Mrs. Scott kill herself?

SUSAN
No one is exactly sure.

JENNA
I don't get why someone would do that.

mc: Mark Moses was the guest star in the very first episode of *The Golden Girls* I ever wrote. This was fifteen years ago and I remember going to that taping. Mark was in his late twenties and I always remembered Mark as being part of that tremendous first experience. I later cast him as one of the husbands on *The Five Mrs. Buchanans*. And he did a guest part for me on my next series, *The Crew*. Mark is just one of those actors who is always so good.

mc: A director or an ABC or Touchstone executive gave me the note that if Susan's divorce was just a year ago, then the pain would be fresher.

mc: We changed Jenna to Julie for clearance.

SUSAN
Well, sometimes people can be so
desperately unhappy they think it's
the only way to solve their problems.

JENNA
But Mrs. Scott always seemed happy.

SUSAN
Yes, but some people pretend to be
one way on the outside when they're
completely different on the inside
because ... well, it's sorta hard to
explain.

JENNA
You mean like how Dad's new
girlfriend is always smiling and
says nice things but deep down you
just know she's a bitch.

SUSAN
I don't like that word, Jenna.
     (then)
But, yes, that is a great example.

INT. SCOTT HOUSE - DINING ROOM - DAY

PEOPLE are milling about, TALKING.
Susan crosses through and places her
MACARONI AND CHEESE on the dining room
table. She removes the foil, BALLS it
up, and crosses to the KITCHEN.

INT. SCOTT HOUSE - KITCHEN - CONTINUOUS

BREE and GABRIELLE are at the table,
each drinking a GLASS OF WINE. There
is an open bottle next to them.
LYNETTE is off to the side BREAST-
FEEDING her toddler.

Susan ENTERS. She throws the balled-up
foil into a TRASH CAN, then crosses to
the table and SITS. The four women sit
in SILENCE, lost in their own thoughts.
Susan then reaches over and picks a
wine GLASS off the table. She STARES at
it for a moment.

CLOSE on the wine glass. Suddenly WINE
is poured into it. We pull back to see
the wine is being poured by MARY ALICE.

We're in a FLASHBACK. It's TWO YEARS
earlier.

SUSAN is sitting in the same chair,
holding the wine GLASS. GABRIELLE and
BREE are seated next to her. LYNETTE
is off to the side. She is eight-months

PREGNANT. MARY ALICE finishes pouring
the wine.

MARY ALICE
There you go, sweetie.

BREE
You want a handkerchief, Susan? I've
got one in my purse.

SUSAN
I'm fine. Really.

Bree begins DIGGING into her purse.
She finds a HANDKERCHIEF and OFFERS it
to Susan.

BREE
It's one of my good ones.
     (proudly)
And see the lace? I tatted it myself.

LYNETTE
First of all, no one's impressed that
you tat your own lace. If anything,
it's weird. Secondly, Susan doesn't
need a hankie. She's not even
crying.

BREE
I don't see why not. If Rex had
cheated on me, I'd be hysterical.

GABRIELLE
So what did Karl say when you
confronted him?

SUSAN
You'll love this. He looked me
straight in the eye and said "It
didn't mean anything."

All the women GROAN.

LYNETTE
What is that? Page one of the
philanderer's handbook?

SUSAN
Then I asked him why he would
jeopardize our marriage like
this? And he just got this Zen look
on his face and said, "You know,
Susan, most men lead lives of quiet
desperation."

GABRIELLE
Oh, I could just hurl.

MC: Several lines in this
scene wound up being
given to other characters.
Once I start to hear the
voices in my head it
becomes harder to switch
jokes between characters
but I was still finding
the voices back then.
In subsequent drafts I
was also trying to make
it clear that Mary Alice was
the center of the wheel
among the housewives.

MC: This flashback scene
was originally much
longer because it was my
first draft and with a lot
of first drafts you're
throwing everything in.
Later you writing for a
page length and you're
have to make sure that you
have no more lines than
you absolutely need.

167

SUSAN
I said, "Really? And what do most women lead? Lives of noisy fulfillment?"

BREE
Good for you.

SUSAN
Sure, we've had our rough patches, but did he have to bang his secretary? My god, I had that woman over for brunch!

GABRIELLE
It's like my grandma said, "An erect penis doesn't have a conscience."

MC: I was working so hard to make Mary Alice so strong and at a certain point I thought, *A little goes a long way.*

MC: One of my comedy writer friends, John Pardee, who is now a writer on the show, read this line and said, "When you say the line aloud the word 'flaccid' doesn't hit." Limp had a funnier cadence.

LYNETTE
Let's be honest. Even the flaccid ones aren't that ethical.

BREE
This is half the reason I joined the NRA. When Rex started going to those education conferences, I wanted it in the back of his mind that he had a loving wife at home with a loaded Smith and Wesson.

MARY ALICE
Lynnie, Tom's always away on business. Do you ever worry he might ... ?

LYNETTE
Please. The man's gotten me pregnant three times in four years. I wish he was having sex with someone else.

BREE
Susan, what are you going to do?

SUSAN
I called a lawyer this morning.

GABRIELLE
Oh, sweetie.

SUSAN
If he was begging my forgiveness, it would be one thing, but he doesn't even seem sorry.

Susan starts to CRY. Bree turns to Lynette.

BREE
(pointedly)
Now can I give her the hankie?

Lynette reacts. Bree HANDS Susan a HANDKERCHIEF.

SUSAN
I'm sorry. It's just ... I don't know how I'm gonna survive this.

Mary Alice REACHES across the table and takes Susan's HAND.

MARY ALICE
I'll tell you how. Whenever it gets so bad you don't think you can take it anymore, you're going to pick up the phone, call us, and we will drop everything and come running.

LYNETTE
Damn straight.

GABRIELLE
Day or night.

BREE
Absolutely.

SUSAN
(touched)
Oh, you guys. You don't have to ...

MARY ALICE
We've all been there. The picket fence routine is a lot harder than it looks. That's why we've got to watch each other's backs.

Susan looks around the room at her friends' SMILING faces. They all BASK for a moment in the GLOW of their FRIENDSHIP.

CLOSE on SUSAN'S FACE.

SHE has a PAINED expression. The FLASHBACK is over.

GABRIELLE (V.O.)
Susan!

SUSAN
What?

GABRIELLE
I said Paul wants us to come over Friday and go through Mary Alice's closet. You know, pack up all her stuff. He can't face doing it himself. I told him we'd be happy to.

SUSAN
Oh. Sure. That's fine.

GABRIELLE
Are you okay?

SUSAN
Yeah. I'm just so ... angry.

BREE
I know. It's such a waste. Mary
Alice was healthy. She had a nice
home. Her family was wonderful. Her
life was ...

LYNETTE
(pointedly)
Our life.

SUSAN
I'm not angry at her. I'm angry at
us. If we'd been paying attention,
maybe we'd have seen there was
a problem. Maybe we could have
helped.

GABRIELLE
I saw her Tuesday. She seemed fine.

SUSAN
Well, obviously something was going
on. And I don't understand why she
couldn't tell us.

LYNETTE
Well ... everyone has their secrets.

Susan looks at Lynette INCREDULOUSLY.

SUSAN
I don't.

LYNETTE
Sure you do.

SUSAN
No, I don't. Not from you guys.

LYNETTE
How can you be thirty-five and not
have any secrets?

SUSAN
I don't know. I just don't.

GABRIELLE
I had a therapist once who said we're
all defined by our secrets.

BREE
Is this the same therapist who made
a pass at you?

GABRIELLE
Yes.

BREE
Well, he should know.

AWKWARD silence. LYNETTE suddenly
lifts her wine GLASS.

LYNETTE
Girls, lift 'em up. I want to
propose a toast.

The other women RAISE their GLASSES.

LYNETTE
To Mary Alice. Whatever was going
on, we hope you've now found peace.

BREE/LYNETTE/SUSAN/GABRIELLE
To Mary Alice.

All the women CLINK their glasses and
sip. Susan wears a slightly TROUBLED
expression.

INT. SCOTT HOUSE - DINING ROOM - A
LITTLE LATER

Susan is placing her MACARONI AND
CHEESE on the buffet table. Jenna is
beside her filling a plate with FOOD.

SUSAN
Jenna, let me ask you something. Is
my life boring?

JENNA
Yeah, but you're a mom. Your life
is supposed to be boring.

Susan STARES at her daughter for a
beat.

SUSAN
Why did I fight so hard to get custody
of you?

JENNA
You were using me to hurt Dad.

SUSAN
Oh, that's right.

Susan AFFECTIONATELY musses Jenna's
hair. Jenna SMILES and crosses away.

Just then, MIKE DELFINO comes up to the
buffet table with an EMPTY plate. Mike
is GOOD-LOOKING in a BLUE-COLLAR sort
of way. Susan WATCHES as he reaches for
the MACARONI AND CHEESE.

MC: James Denton and Teri Hatcher never read together as part of his audition process. I was just holding my breath that they would have chemistry. You could see right from the start that they were pretty darn cute together, but it wasn't really until we got dailies in that you started seeing something about the relationship that just pops off the screen. Right from the start fans responded the way we wanted them to. They wanted them to be together, and you need the audience to feel that for any romantic coupling to work.

10

SUSAN
You don't want to do that.

MIKE
Excuse me?

SUSAN
I'm suggesting you stay away from
the macaroni and cheese.

MIKE
Oh. You had some?

SUSAN
No, I made it.

MIKE
Really?

SUSAN
Yes. Don't ask me how I did it, but
it's unbelievably dreadful.

Mike, completely CHARMED by Susan's
candor, starts to SCOOP a big helping
of the MACARONI AND CHEESE. Susan
STOPS him.

SUSAN
(smiling)
Do you have a death wish? I'm
serious here. It's awful.

MIKE
I refuse to believe anyone could
screw up macaroni and cheese that
badly.

Mike SCOOPS the MACARONI AND CHEESE
onto his plate. He winks at Susan, then
tries some. He instantly GRIMACES.

MIKE
(mouth full)
Omigod! How did you ... ? It tastes
like it's burned *and* undercooked.

SUSAN
I get that a lot.

Susan hands him a NAPKIN. After he
discretely spits out the food, he
looks up at Susan. They both start
to LAUGH. Then:

MIKE
We probably shouldn't be laughing.

SUSAN
It's okay. Mary Alice would've
laughed. She had a great sense of
humor.

MIKE
She's the woman who died?

SUSAN
Yeah. You didn't know her?

MIKE
I just moved to the neighborhood.
Mrs. Huber insisted I come. So I
could meet people.

SUSAN
You moved into the Sims house? I
live across the street. I'm Susan
Meyer.

MIKE
Mike Delfino. Nice to meet you.

SUSAN
(re: macaroni)
Well, now that everyone has seen
that I brought something, I should
probably throw this out.

Susan SMILES at Mike, then crosses
away. She takes a few steps away, then
looks back and is THRILLED to see Mike
is watching her walk away.

INT. SCOTT HOUSE - LIVING ROOM -
CONTINUOUS

Bree, Gabrielle, and Lynette are seated
off to the side. Lynette is trying to
discretely BREASTFEED her toddler,
PATSY. She FLINCHES in pain.

LYNETTE
(to Patsy)
Ow! Ease up, you little vampire!

GABRIELLE
Lynnie, she's almost a year and a
half. Shouldn't you have broken out
the strained peaches by now?

LYNETTE
I'm trying. But I think she's
developed a taste for human flesh.

BREE
I knew this woman back in Alabama.
She breastfed her son til he was
four. Can you imagine? When he was
hungry he would lick his lips, point
at her chest and say, "Tit, please."

MC: The whole trajectory of Mike and Susan's story changed because in this draft I was building to a kiss and they were spending all their time together. When I got rid of the kiss and put in Edie, I had to get all my exposition out so I added what he did for a living. The fact that he's a plumber had to be set up so Edie could make her joke about her pipes.

MC: A female friend told me this story. She met a woman in the south whose four-year-old breastfed. So I put it in. At this point in the process I was working a lot harder at doing *Sex and the City*–type dialogue, where the women talk about shocking things in suburban, domestic topic areas. It was probably for the best that I cut it. Now that the show is going, it's not about the four women getting together and talking. The nature of our show is that the women keep so many secrets from each other that it's hard to get them together talking, which makes the network crazy because they want them together as much as possible.

GABRIELLE
That's how Carlos was the first year of our marriage. Except he wouldn't say, "Please."

Mrs. Huber suddenly crosses over.

MRS. HUBER
Lynette, I've been looking all over for you. Are you aware of what your children are doing?

A look of PANIC crosses Lynette's face.

INT. KITCHEN - SCOTT HOUSE - CONTINUOUS

Susan is DUMPING her macaroni and cheese into a trash can. Jenna ENTERS.

JENNA
Mom, who was that man you were talking to?

SUSAN
That's Mr. Delfino. He just moved in down the street.

JENNA
Really? Well, he's a hottie.

SUSAN
Yes, he is. Jenna, how would you like to do me a favor?

JENNA
You want me to find out if he's single?

SUSAN
Just be subtle like Mommy taught you.

Jenna turns and EXITS.

EXT. SCOTT BACKYARD - DAY

Various MOURNERS are scattered throughout the BACKYARD. In the center is a POOL.

LYNETTE, carrying the baby, emerges from the house to see that her three SONS are in the pool SWIMMING. Three little piles of CLOTHING are at the poll's edge. Lynette RACES over.

LYNETTE
(mortified)
What are you doing? We are at a wake!

PETER
When we got here you said we could go in the pool.

LYNETTE
I said you could go *by* the pool!
(looking closely)
Are you wearing swimsuits?

PETER
Yeah. We put 'em on under our clothes before we left the house.

LYNETTE
So you three *planned* this?
(livid)
That does it. Get out!

PETER/PAUL
No!

LYNETTE
No? No?! I am your mother! You have to do what I say!

PETER
Why?

LYNETTE
(apoplectic)
Why?! Because that's how it works!!!

The twins CROSS their ARMS in DEFIANCE. PRESTON looks over at his brothers, then crosses his arms as well. LYNETTE, helpless, stares at them in SHOCK. She then looks up.

LYNETTE'S POV: EVERYONE in the BACKYARD is watching, waiting to see what she will do.

MARY ALICE (V.O.)
Suddenly, Lynette was aware that everyone was staring at her. What's worse, they were judging her. So she decided, in a split second, to do something that would be talked about on Wisteria Lane for years to come.

LYNETTE suddenly thrusts her toddler into a stranger's arms. She then slowly DESCENDS down into the POOL. She WADES over to an ASTONISHED Peter and Paul and GRABS them both by the ear. She FORCES them out of the pool. She then throws back a look at Preston, who quickly SCURRIES out of the pool.

FELICITY HUFFMAN: We reshot the pool scene because Marc cleverly wanted a shot of my legs under the water. He needed a close-up when I was going, "Get out of the pool, get out of the pool." He wanted an intimate feeling of her being caught between a rock and a hard place. I had to shoot it twice. It was all day, getting in and out of the pool. Those boys are fantastic and they're all over the place. They kept swimming to the other end of the pool and I couldn't swim in my big dress.

Lynette PICKS up the boys' clothing, SHOVES it into their arms, and gestures for them to EXIT. They do. Lynette then takes her toddler from the stranger and crosses over, SOAKING WET, to an astonished Mr. Scott.

> LYNETTE
> (totally dignified)
> Paul, we have to leave now. Once again, I'm so sorry for your loss.

Lynette then turns and CROSSES away. All the ASTONISHED mourners watch her as she goes.

INT. MEYER HOUSE - BEDROOM - THE NEXT MORNING

Susan is ASLEEP. Jenna ENTERS and JUMPS on the bed. She SHAKES Susan's arm.

> JENNA
> Get up. I want pancakes for breakfast.

> SUSAN
> (eyes shut)
> I'm still asleep, honey. Just make yourself some cereal.

> JENNA
> Come on. We've got maple syrup.

> SUSAN
> Good. Use it on the cereal.

> JENNA
> (pointedly)
> I saw Mrs. Huber this morning while she was walking her dog and I found out some stuff about Mr. Delfino.

Susan RAISES her head.

> SUSAN
> What stuff?

> JENNA
> Well, he's a plumber. And he makes a lot of money. He's got a kid named Timmy that goes to my school. And his wife died six months ago.

Susan STARES at Jenna for a BEAT, then gets up out of the bed and HEADS toward the kitchen.

> JENNA
> And, remember, I like blueberries in my pancakes.

> SUSAN
> I know.

Susan EXITS. Jenna SMILES as she watches her go.

INT. SOLIS HOUSE - KITCHEN - CONTINUOUS

Carlos and Gabrielle are in the middle of a FIGHT.

> GABRIELLE
> Tonight? We're going to the Tanakas' tonight? Why am I just hearing about this now?!

> CARLOS
> It's a business thing. It just came up! I'll need you ready by seven.

> GABRIELLE
> You're always springing stuff like this on me! What if I had plans?

> CARLOS
> Right. Like your life is so full.

Carlos EXITS. Gabrielle SMOLDERS.

> CARLOS
> John!

> JOHN
> (in pain)
> Ow! Mr. Solis, you scared me.

> CARLOS
> (pointing to bush)
> Why is that bush still here? You were supposed to dig that up last week.

> JOHN
> Well, I didn't have time last week cause I had to ...

> CARLOS
> (menacingly)
> I don't want to hear your excuses, John. Just take care of the bush.

> JOHN
> (cowed)
> Yes, Mr. Solis.

CARLOS crosses to his car. GABRIELLE emerges from the house.

> GABRIELLE
> Carlos, why should I help you out considering how you always treat me?

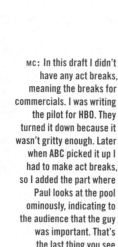

MC: In this draft I didn't have any act breaks, meaning the breaks for commercials. I was writing the pilot for HBO. They turned it down because it wasn't gritty enough. Later when ABC picked it up I had to make act breaks, so I added the part where Paul looks at the pool ominously, indicating to the audience that the guy was important. That's the last thing you see before the first commercial.

MC: Jesse Metcalfe came onboard after the original pilot had been shot. The original John looked like a young slender 16-year-old, perfectly attractive, but not a sex god, more like a young, shy teenager. It was a much more dangerous casting choice. When we tested the Gabrielle-John scenes with audiences, people didn't get why Gabrielle would be cheating on her husband with this young boy. And a couple of my gay friends specifically said, "No, you've done this wrong. You have to cast a complete hunk so that people know why she's cheating on her husband. And also, we could use some eye candy for the series." So we cast Jesse. Of course, it turned out to be the correct decision. People said, 'Okay, she's using him for sex. He can fall in love with her, and he looks like a man, so we're not worried about it.

CARLOS
You want a reason? I paid fifty
thousand for your Lexus. I paid four
thousand for your necklace. And I
paid two thousand for your lipo. All
together that's ...

Carlos pauses.

GABRIELLE
(he's so stupid)
Fifty-six.

CARLOS
Fifty-six thousand reasons.
(then)
So can I tell Tanaka we'll be there?

GABRIELLE sees that John is BLEEDING.

GABRIELLE
John, is that blood?

JOHN
I cut myself on some thorns.

GABRIELLE
We have come Bactine and bandages on
the top shelf in the kitchen.

JOHN
Thank you, Mrs. Solis.

John EXITS into the house. GABRIELLE
turns back to Carlos.

GABRIELLE
I can't be ready before seven-
thirty.

CARLOS
(suddenly smiling)
See? This is what marriage is all
about. Compromise.

Carlos gets into his CAR. Gabrielle
WATCHES him drive off, then heads BACK
into the house.

INT. SOLIS HOUSE - KITCHEN - CONTINUOUS

John is finishing wrapping a BANDAGE on
his finger. GABRIELLE enters.

GABRIELLE
Is your finger okay?

JOHN
It's fine. It was just a small cut.

GABRIELLE crosses to JOHN. She takes
him by the HAND. She examines it for a
beat. Suddenly she KISSES his FINGER.

She then GRABS his head with both
of her HANDS and starts to kiss him
PASSIONATELY. He starts kissing her
back. Suddenly, he PULLS back.

JOHN
You know, Mrs. Solis, I really enjoy
it when we hook up, but ... you know,
I gotta get my work done. I can't
afford to lose this job and ...

Gabrielle UNBUTTONS her blouse and
lets it DROP to the floor. John,
overcome by the sight of her BODY,
drops his TOOLS.

Gabrielle QUICKLY takes John by the
hand and LEADS him into the DINING
room. She points to the dining room
table.

GABRIELLE
This table is hand-carved. Carlos
had it imported from Italy. It cost
him fifteen thousand dollars.

JOHN
You want to do it on the table this
time?

GABRIELLE
Absolutely.

John PICKS Gabrielle up and LAYS her on
top of the TABLE. He pulls his SHIRT
off, then GETS on the table with her.
They kiss for a beat, then John begins
LAUGHING.

GABRIELLE
What?

JOHN
The last thing your husband said to
me was to make sure I took care of
the bush.

GABRIELLE
(laughing)
He really should learn to be more
specific.

Gabrielle and John lay back on the
table. The camera pans up to reveal
the CHINA CABINET behind them.

RICARDO ANTONIO CHAVIRA:
I ran into a buddy of mine,
an actor friend, who had
gone in for the show prior
to me. I had just gotten
back from doing a play in
Seattle and my buddy came
to me and said, "Dude, I
just auditioned for this
thing. It's not me but you
are perfect for it." He still
had the sides in his hand.
It was the scene where I
say, "If he wants to grab
your ass, you let him." I
said, "Oh, he's a total jerk,
so I'm perfect for it.
Thanks." But I know that I
can pull off these roles.
I went in on the last day
that they were seeing
people. I dressed up in a
suit, walked in, and did my
stuff. Marc Cherry had this
look on his face. It looked
like his mouth was a little
open. He was looking at me
like, "Where have you been
for three weeks?"

MC: I liked the line about
the bush but it went away
because I was being
protective of tonality for a
network TV show. It stayed
in through subsequent
drafts and it was right
before we were going to
shoot it that it got cut.

173

It pushes in on a RED plate that is displayed on the center shelf.

INT. VAN DE KAMP HOUSE - DINING ROOM - NIGHT

We open on a BLUE plate that is displayed on the center shelf of a CHINA CABINET.

We pull back to reveal we're now in the VAN DE KAMP dining room. BREE and REX sit at opposite ends of the table. In the middle are their fifteen-year-old son, ANDREW, and their thirteen-year-old daughter, DANIELLE. They are all QUIETLY eating dinner at an ELEGANTLY set table.

DANIELLE looks up from her BOWL.

                DANIELLE
    Why can't we ever have normal soup?

                BREE
    Danielle, there is nothing abnormal
    about basil purée.

                DANIELLE
    But just once couldn't we have
    something people have heard of?
    Like French onion or Navy bean?

                BREE
    First of all, your father can't eat
    onions. He's deathly allergic. And
    I won't even dignify your Navy bean
    suggestion.
        (then, cheerily)
    So how does everyone like their osso
    buco?

                ANDREW
        (indifferent)
    It's okay.

Bree GENTLY places her fork on her plate.

                BREE
    You know, Andrew, I spent four hours
    cooking this meal. How do you think
    it makes me feel when you say "it's
    okay" in that sullen tone?

                ANDREW
    Well, who asked you to spend four
    hours on dinner?

                BREE
    Excuse me?

                ANDREW
    Corey Harper's mom gets home from
    the office, pops open a can of pork
    and beans, and boom! They're
    eating. Everyone's happy.

Long beat.

                BREE
        (coldly)
    Pork and beans.

                DANIELLE
        (sotto, to Andrew)
    Apologize now. I'm begging.

                BREE
    You'd rather I serve pork and beans?!

                ANDREW
    I'm just saying does every dinner
    have to be one of Martha Stewart's
    greatest hits?

Bree throws her NAPKIN down on the TABLE. She quickly rises and begins PACING around the room. She suddenly CROSSES to Andrew and LEANS into him.

                BREE
    You're doing drugs, aren't you?

                ANDREW
    What?!

                BREE
    Change in behavior is one of the
    warning signs and you've been as
    fresh as paint for the past six
    months. So is it crack? That would
    certainly explain why you're always
    locked in the bathroom.

                DANIELLE
    Trust me. That's not what he's doing
    in the bathroom.

                ANDREW
        (to Danielle)
    Shut up!
        (to Bree)
    Mom, I'm not the problem here.
    You're the one always acting like
    she's running for the mayor of
    Stepford.

                BREE
    Hey! I work myself to the point of
    exhaustion to create a lifestyle for
    my family that is both elegant and
    wholesome. And it's astonishing to

MC: Charles McDougall had said to me when we were shooting the pilot that we should take out pop cultural references so the pilot had more of a timeless feel. And I reluctantly agreed to that. I loved referencing Martha Stewart because I thought she was the epitome of what desperate housewives aspire to, the woman who seemingly had it all together. But I thought Charles had a good point, which is that the attitudes and actions of these women could play in any era.

JOY LAUREN: It took me a couple minutes to get what that line, "Trust me, that is not what he's doing," meant. When I realized, I thought, *Oh my God.* But that's just who he is and she just wants to be honest about it. I did get a kick out of saying it. They laughed at the audition when I said it.

me that the only reaction I get for my effort is cold indifference.

              ANDREW
     Whatever.

Andrew sullenly resumes EATING. Bree SITS back down. Beat.

              BREE
     Rex, seeing how you're head of this household, I would really appreciate you saying something.

Rex LOOKS UP from his food.

              REX
     Kids, how'd you like to go out tomorrow night and have cheeseburgers that are dripping with fat and grease?

              DANIELLE
     Sounds great.

              ANDREW
     Thanks, Dad.

Bree STARES at Rex in utter SHOCK. Rex gives her a look of complete DISDAIN. After a beat, the entire family resumes eating their food in SILENCE.

INT. MEYER HOUSE - KITCHEN - NIGHT

CLOSE ON A CAN OF PORK AND BEANS.

Susan picks the CAN up from the COUNTER and begins to open it with a CAN OPENER. Jenna is at the kitchen TABLE making a FORT out of POPSICLE STICKS.

              SUSAN
     I can't do it! I'd be too nervous.

              JENNA
     Mom, if you want to date Mr. Delfino, you're gonna have to ask him out. It's the only way.

              SUSAN
     Well, maybe he'll ask me out.

              JENNA
     Please. I'll be dating before that happens.

              SUSAN
     Okay. Yes, I'll probably have to make the first move. But, to be honest, I'm not sure if I'm even ready to start dating.

              JENNA
     Come on. You need to get back out there. How long has it been since you've had sex?

Susan turns and STARES at Jenna for a long beat.

              JENNA
     Are you mad that I asked that?

              SUSAN
     No, I'm trying to remember.
       (off Jenna's fort)
     So this is for school, huh? When I was in fifth grade I made the White House out of sugar cubes.

              JENNA
     Stop changing the subject! Go over there right now and ask him out.

              SUSAN
     First, I'm not going to be goaded into dating Mr. Delfino. Secondly, I don't want to talk about my love life with you anymore. It weirds me out.

              JENNA
     Sorry. I wouldn't have brought it up. It's just ...

              SUSAN
     What?

              JENNA
     I heard Dad's girlfriend ask if you'd had sex with anyone since the divorce and Dad said he doubted it.

Susan looks at Jenna, STUNNED.

              JENNA
     And then they both laughed.

EXT. STREET - A FEW MOMENTS LATER

A DETERMINED Susan is striding across the STREET. She quickly walks up to Mike who is in his front yard planting FLOWERS.

              MIKE
     Hey, Susan! What's up?

              SUSAN
       (playfully)
     I was wondering if you were ready for more of my macaroni and cheese.

175

MC: Susan's last name was spelled Meyer until the pilot was picked up. Then changed to Mayer for clearance purposes.

MIKE
My stomach's got to be pumped two
more times, then I'm good to go.

SUSAN
Great.
    (off flowers)
Are those zinnias?

MIKE
    (nodding)
Yeah. The woman on the corner
brought them. As a housewarming
gift.

SUSAN
Oh. That's Evie McCall. She just
got divorced.

MIKE
She told me. Then she invited me to
her house so she could show me her
zamioculcus.

SUSAN
Is that a plant?

MIKE
God, I hope so.
    (wryly)
It's unbelievable. Ever since I
moved in I have been hit on by every
divorcée in a three block radius.

Susan STARES at him with a smile FROZEN
on her face. She's SCREWED. She begins
thinking FURIOUSLY. Suddenly:

SUSAN
    (eureka!)
I have a clog?

MIKE
Excuse me?

SUSAN
    (too enthusiastic)
Uh ... that's why I came over. I have
a clog and you're a plumber. Right?!

MIKE
Yeah.

SUSAN
The clog is in a pipe.

MIKE
Yes. That's usually where they are.

SUSAN
Well, I got one.

MC: The character of Evie,
or Edie, got bigger in
subsequent drafts. It
occurred to me that if I
played up the rivalry it
would increase Susan's
desperation. Once the
decision was made that
Susan burns down Edie's
house, I had to make Edie
more of a threat. In this
draft Susan doesn't really
have a defining scene the
way the other women do:
Gabrielle with the
lawnmower, Bree crying in
the bathroom, Lynette
going into the pool. I
worked with John Pardee
and Joey Murphy, who in
addition to being writers on
my show are also close
friends. We were thinking,
*What's a desperate act for
a woman who's interested
in a guy?* and we came up
with the idea of her going
to the house where she
thinks he is, another
woman's house. She walks
in, there are candles lit,
she assumes they're
screwing and knocks over
a candle accidentally. Once
I had that as my major
thing, which I knew would
be great, we had to
restructure Susan's story
to build up to it.

176

MIKE
Okay. Well ... I'll go get my tools.

SUSAN
    (panicked)
Now? You want to come now?!

MIKE
Well, I'm not doing anything. Give
me two minutes and I'll be right
over.

Mike goes inside and SHUTS the door.
Susan remains FROZEN for a beat, then
BOLTS back to her house.

INT. MEYER HOUSE - KITCHEN

Susan is FURIOUSLY pulling HAIR out
of three HAIR BRUSHES. She SHOVES the
hair at Jenna who is HURRIEDLY stuffing
it down the kitchen sink DRAIN.

SUSAN
That's it! Just stuff the hair down
there. All the way down!

JENNA
This is as far as my arm goes!

SUSAN
Wait. Do we have peanut butter?!
Mixed with hair that should clog
really good!

Susan RUSHES to the pantry and begins
looking inside.

JENNA
We just bought the peanut butter.

SUSAN
    (looking)
We'll buy more!

Jenna turns on the FAUCET.

JENNA
Mom, we're gonna need something
else. This isn't clogging!

SFX: DOORBELL

SUSAN
    (freaked)
Omigod! That's him! Dammit! How am
I gonna stop up this sink?!!

Susan and Jenna FRANTICALLY look
around the room. They suddenly see
SOMETHING.

CLOSE ON JENNA'S POPSICLE FORT.

Susan and Jenna SLOWLY look at each
other. A look of DISMAY suddenly
crosses Jenna's FACE.

INT. MEYER HOUSE - KITCHEN - A LITTLE
LATER

MIKE is working UNDER the SINK. Susan
is sitting on the floor next to him.

> MIKE
> Here's the problem. It looks like
> someone stuffed a bunch of popsicle
> sticks down here.

> SUSAN
> (innocently)
> I've told Jenna a million times not
> to play in the kitchen. I don't know
> what I'm gonna do with her.

Jenna POKES her head into the kitchen.
She GLARES at Susan. Susan mouths "I'M
SORRY" to her. Jenna shakes her head
in DISGUST.

INT. SUPERMARKET - DAY

Susan and Lynette are WALKING side-by-
side. Susan CARRIES a small grocery
BASKET.

Lynette is PUSHING one shopping CART
filled with groceries. Her toddler,
PATSY, is in the front seat. Behind her
she PULLS a SECOND cart that contains
PETER, PAUL and PRESTON.

> SUSAN
> So ... you'll be thrilled to know I'm
> not a typically boring housewife
> anymore.

> LYNETTE
> You're not?

> SUSAN
> No. I finally have a secret.

> LYNETTE
> A secret?

> SUSAN
> Remember at the wake I said I didn't
> have any secrets. I now have one.

> LYNETTE
> Well, good for you.

Patsy TUGS at her mother's SLEEVE.

> PATSY
> Ball.

> SUSAN
> Omigosh! Did Patsy just say "ball?"

> LYNETTE
> Yep. It's her first word. She says it
> while pointing at food, furniture,
> plants, and our dog. Once she says
> it in the presence of an actual ball
> I'll get excited.
> (then)
> So can you at least give me a hint
> about the secret?

> SUSAN
> (proudly)
> It concerns my love life.

> LYNETTE
> Oh. Is this about the little crush
> you have on Mike Delfino?

> SUSAN
> How the heck did you ... ?

> LYNETTE
> Edith Huber saw you talking to him
> outside his house. She said you had
> a goofy look on your face.

Patsy points to an ITEM on the SHELF.

> PATSY
> Ball.

> LYNETTE
> No, sweetie. Those are tampons.

> SUSAN
> I hate Edith Huber.

> LYNETTE
> So did you ask him out?

> SUSAN
> Not yet.

> LYNETTE
> You better get a move on. Evie
> McCall just got her legs waxed which
> means she is open for business.

> SUSAN
> It's just Karl did such a number on
> my self-esteem. I keep feeling like
> Mike is out of my league.

MICHAEL EDELSTEIN
(EXECUTIVE PRODUCER):
I waited a while through
the casting process to
introduce Marc and Jamie
Denton. Jamie and I had
worked on *Threat Matrix*
together and when I
brought him in, Marc just
loved him, and Charles
McDougall, the director of
the pilot, loved him. I feel
very vindicated now. Three
TV Guide covers later, I've
been proven right about
him. It's funny because
after it became clear that
Threat Matrix was not going
to make it, I said to Jamie,
"I think the show is going to
be cancelled but the truth
is, you never know why
people come into each
other's lives. Maybe we
were supposed to meet on
this show for something
we're going to do in the
future." That's what
happened.

LYNETTE
You are gorgeous, smart, and funny.
He would be lucky to date you.

SUSAN
Thanks. I needed that. Listen, I'm
gonna head over to aisle three. I
gotta buy a whole bunch of popsicles.

Susan CROSSES away. Lynette continues
down the aisle. A woman in a
WHEELCHAIR passes by. Patsy POINTS to
the woman.

PATSY
Ball.

LYNETTE
No, sweetie. That's a paraplegic.

As Lynette is TURNING the corner she
hears:

WOMAN'S VOICE (O.S.)
Lynette Scavo! Is that you?

Lynette looks around to see NATALIE
WELLMAN, a thirty-ish woman in a
TAILORED suit, standing a few feet
away.

LYNETTE
Natalie Wellman? I don't believe it.

NATALIE
How long has it been? Six years?

LYNETTE
At least. I haven't seen you since I
quit the firm. How are things?

NATALIE
Fine. Remember how we always
called Mr. Kerns "head sonofabitch"
behind his back? Well, over the
weekend someone stenciled "head
sonofabitch" on his parking spot.

LYNETTE
(amused)
Do they have any idea who did it?

NATALIE
Actually, it was me. But I'm letting
the guy in the mailroom take the
fall.

LYNETTE
(wistful)
"Head sonofabitch." I'd forgotten
about that.

NATALIE
Wow. Just look at you. You look like
an actual mom.

LYNETTE
This surprises you?

NATALIE
It's just ... you were the corporate
golden girl. Rising through the
ranks so quickly. Everyone thought
you'd be running the company by now.
And to just walk away from it all ...

LYNETTE
(clearly uncomfortable)
Yeah, well ...

NATALIE
But I'm sure this is so much more
fulfilling. So ... do you just love
being a mom?

Before Lynette can speak, there is a
loud CRASH. Lynette and Natalie react.
STARTLED. Lynette turns to see that
the SHOPPING CART that contained her
three sons is now EMPTY.

Lynette turns back to Natalie.

LYNETTE
Will you excuse me for a moment?

Before Natalie can respond, Lynette
QUICKLY plops Patsy into the empty
shopping cart and quickly PACES down
the aisle.

As she turns into the next aisle,
Lynette sees the FLOOR is STREWN with
SOUP CANS everywhere. She looks up and
sees her three sons STANDING on the top
SHELF.

LYNETTE
(horrified)
What in God's name ... ?!

PAUL
We were trying to help you shop.

LYNETTE
Oh, for God's ... ! Just get down!
Now!

All three boys start to CLIMB down.

LYNETTE
Look at the mess you've made! We
have to clean this up!

Lynette and the three boys get down on their KNEES and begin picking up CANS. A manager comes RUNNING up.

> LYNETTE
> (to manager)
> I'm so sorry. My kids knocked down your shelves. We're cleaning it up.

> GROCERY STORE MANAGER
> (annoyed)
> That's okay. I'll take care of it.

> LYNETTE
> We don't mind.

> GROCERY STORE MANAGER
> (coldly)
> Please.

Lynette, HUMILIATED, gets up and motions for the boys to move. As they're all CROSSING away, they pass two MIDDLE-AGED WOMEN who have witnessed EVERYTHING.

> MIDDLE-AGED WOMAN
> (to her friend)
> I tell you, some people just refuse to control their children.

Lynette, who has OVERHEARD this, stops. She turns and CROSSES to the woman.

> LYNETTE
> Excuse me? What did you just say?

> MIDDLE-AGED WOMAN
> (taken aback)
> Nothing.

> LYNETTE
> (with increasing fervor)
> You know, this isn't easy! My husband is always away on business. My baby-sitter has joined the Witness Relocation Program. Which means I'm doing it all by myself! Four kids all under the age of seven! It's not easy! And everything considered, I think I'm doing a bang-up job!

Lynette notices that EVERYONE in the aisle is WATCHING.

> LYNETTE
> Got that everybody?! I'm doing a good job! I am a good mother!!

Suddenly Patsy TUGS at her mother's sleeve and SAYS:

> PATSY
> Sonofabitch.

A look of utter MORTIFICATION crosses Lynette's face. She turns, totally defeated, and walks past the ASTOUNDED SHOPPERS.

EXT. SOLIS HOUSE - FRONT YARD - NIGHT

Carlos, still in his business SUIT, is bent over PEERING closely at the LAWN. Gabrielle EMERGES from the front door. She is DRESSED in a stunning evening GOWN.

> GABRIELLE
> I found my earrings. We can go now.
> (off Carlos)
> What are you doing?

> CARLOS
> (still looking at lawn)
> Was John here today?

> GABRIELLE
> Yes.

> CARLOS
> I don't think he mowed this lawn.

> GABRIELLE
> Of course he did.

Carlos gets down on his KNEES. He starts feeling the GRASS.

> CARLOS
> Feel this. He did not mow this lawn! What does he do when he's here?

> GABRIELLE
> (getting nervous)
> Carlos, we're going to be late.

> CARLOS
> Screw him. We're getting a new gardener.

> GABRIELLE
> (alarmed)
> A new gardener? Why?

Carlos turns and looks at Gabrielle
> CARLOS
> Are you deaf? I just said he's not doing his job?

179

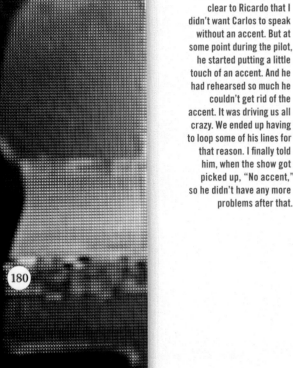

GABRIELLE
(back-pedaling)
Fine. Hire whoever you want. It's just ... I think you're being unfair to John. He works very hard. Trust me.

MC: I had never made it clear to Ricardo that I didn't want Carlos to speak without an accent. But at some point during the pilot, he started putting a little touch of an accent. And he had rehearsed so much he couldn't get rid of the accent. It was driving us all crazy. We ended up having to loop some of his lines for that reason. I finally told him, when the show got picked up, "No accent," so he didn't have any more problems after that.

CARLOS
Then why isn't the yardwork done?!

GABRIELLE
It's dark. You just can't see that the lawn has been mowed.

CARLOS
It hasn't! Feel this grass.

GABRIELLE
Carlos, I really don't think we should be late. We can talk about this in the morning. Okay?

ANNOYED, Carlos turns and HEADS for the car. An INTENSE look comes over Gabrielle's FACE as she watches him go.

INT. TANAKA HOUSE - ENTRY HALL - A LITTLE LATER

A SWANK party with WELL-DRESSED men and women milling about. A waiter PASSES through with DRINKS on a tray. Carlos and Gabrielle ENTER the front door. Carlos immediately SPOTS an elderly JAPANESE gentleman who waves him over.

CARLOS
There's Tanaka. Time for me to go into my dance.

GABRIELLE
Sweetie, wait. I need the car keys. I left my purse in the front seat.

Carlos DIGS into his pocket and hands Gabrielle the KEYS. He then heads into the PARTY.

Gabrielle WATCHES him cross away, then GRABS the waiter as he is PASSING by her.

GABRIELLE
(to waiter)
That's my husband over there. Can you make sure he's got a drink in his hand all night long?

Gabrielle HANDS the waiter a TWENTY dollar bill.

WAITER
Yes, ma'am.

Gabrielle smiles. She then turns and EXITS the front door.

INT. CAR - MOMENTS LATER

Gabrielle is SPEEDING through the neighborhood with an INTENSE look on her face.

EXT. SOLIS HOUSE - DRIVEWAY - MOMENTS LATER

The garage door LIFTS up automatically. Gabrielle QUICKLY pulls up and JUMPS out of the car. She DISAPPEARS into the garage. A few moments later she APPEARS pushing the LAWN MOWER.

EXT. SOLIS HOUSE - FRONT YARD - A WHILE LATER

Gabrielle, still in her evening GOWN, is hurriedly MOWING the lawn.

EXT. SOLIS HOUSE - FRONT YARD - A WHILE LATER

Gabrielle is FURIOUSLY trimming her hedge.

Across the street, a man in a BATHROBE pulls his trash CAN to the curb. He looks up to see Gabrielle doing YARD WORK in her GOWN. He looks down at his own SHABBY bathrobe and SLIPPERS. He self-consciously PULLS his bathrobe TIGHTER, then EXITS back into his home.

INT. TANAKA HOUSE - LIVING ROOM - A LITTLE LATER

Gabrielle SLIPS in. Calm and collected, she immediately LOOKS for Carlos.

She CROSSES into the living room and sees Carlos standing in a group of men. He is LAUGHING uproariously. He is obviously DRUNK.

As Gabrielle is watching, the waiter crosses up and takes the GLASS from Carlos's hand and REPLACES it with another. Carlos doesn't NOTICE.

INT. SOLIS HOUSE - LIVING ROOM - NEXT MORNING

Gabrielle is sipping COFFEE, reading the PAPER. Carlos emerges from the bedroom putting on his JACKET. He is clearly suffering from a HANGOVER.

>   CARLOS
> Why the hell did you let me drink so much last night?

>   GABRIELLE
> I was so busy talking to the other wives I didn't even notice. I'm glad you had a good time.

>   CARLOS
> I must have been wasted. I don't even remember how I got home last night.

>   GABRIELLE
> Don't worry. I drove. So what would you like for dinner tonight?

>   CARLOS
> Food is the last thing I want to talk about right now. I'll call you later.

>   GABRIELLE
>   (demurely)
> I'll be here.

Gabrielle GIVES Carlos a PECK on the cheek. He forces a SMILE then WALKS out the front door. Gabrielle WAITS for a beat, then RUNS to the window.

EXT. SOLID HOUSE - FRONT YARD - CONTINUOUS

Carlos is in the middle of the walkway staring down at the LAWN, which has obviously been MOWED.

He bends down to FEEL it. He stands up, thoroughly CONFUSED.

CLOSE on GABRIELLE who's watching from the window. She SMILES.

INT. FAST-FOOD RESTAURANT - DAY

Bree, Rex, Andrew, and Danielle are seated at a BOOTH. A WAITRESS is standing beside them, waiting for their ORDERS.

>   ANDREW
>   I want the chili dog combo platter.
>   DANIELLE
> I'll have the double-decker burger. And potato skins for an appetizer.

>   REX
> Deluxe patty melt with home fries.

>   WAITRESS
>   (to Bree)
> And how about you?

>   BREE
> I'll have bottled water and a lemon wedge.

>   WAITRESS
> We're out of lemons.

>   BREE
> Of course you are.

The waitress takes everyone's MENU and crosses away. Andrew looks across the room.

>   ANDREW
> Hey, they got video games! Is it okay if we play until our food gets here?

>   BREE
> This is family time, Andrew. I don't think ...

>   REX
>   (interrupting)
> Go ahead and play.

Bree GIVES Rex a look. The KIDS leave the booth. Beat.

>   BREE
> I know you think I'm angry about coming here tonight. But I'm not.

Rex STARES at Bree and says nothing.

>   BREE
> You and the kids want a change of pace. Something fun. I get it.

Rex continues to STARE at her.

>   BREE
>   (uneasy)
> But I do think tomorrow night we'll all want to cleanse our palates with something healthier. I'm thinking about serving chicken Saltimbocca.

Rex says nothing and continues to STARE. Bree carries on.
>   BREE
>   (clearly uncomfortable)

22

With carrots. And maybe a peach
tart for dessert. Doesn't that
sound good?

                    REX
          I want a divorce.

Bree, shocked, stares at him.

                    REX
          I just can't live in a freaking
          detergent commercial anymore.

                    BREE
          I don't know what you mean.

                    REX
          Of course you don't.

The waitress walks up and sets a PLATE
in front of Rex.

                    WAITRESS
          This is for the salad bar.

                    REX
          Thank you.

The waitress LEAVES. Rex and Bree sit
in SILENCE for a beat.

                    BREE
               (suddenly)
          Why don't I get your salad for you?

                    REX
          Bree ...

Bree CROSSES to the salad bar. As she
starts putting together a salad, an
attractive woman, EVIE McCALL, walks
over.

                    EVIE
          Bree, is that you?

                    BREE
               (surprised)
          Evie McCall! Hi! How are you?

                    EVIE
          My divorce lawyer was ruthless. I'm
          great. How are things with you?

                    BREE
          Things?

                    EVIE
          Yeah. Is everything good?

MC: Some of Evie's lines
were given to Mrs. Huber. I
had to keep Mrs. Huber
alive in the pilot as much
as possible, because I
realized I was going to
have her in the series.

Bree LOOKS at her for a long beat.
WANTING to tell her the truth. But she
CAN'T.

                    BREE
               (with a big smile)
          Everything is great. Just great.

                    EVIE
          Oh, I'm so glad.

                    BREE
          I'll call you. We'll have lattes.

Bree crosses BACK to the table. She
sets the salad plate DOWN in front of
Rex and SITS.

                    BREE
          I got you the honey mustard
          dressing. Their Thousand Island
          looked a little suspect.

A beat of silence. Rex starts to eat
his SALAD. Then:

                    REX
          Want to talk about what I just said?

                    BREE
               (angrily)
          If you think I'm going to discuss
          the dissolution of my marriage in
          a place where the restrooms are
          labeled "Chicks" and "Dudes," you
          are out of your mind. Now eat your
          salad.

Rex continues EATING. Suddenly, a
strange LOOK comes over his FACE. He
drops his fork, then GRABS his throat.
Bree looks up.

                    BREE
          What is it? What's wrong?

                    REX
               (re: salad)
          What's in this?

                    BREE
          What do you mean, "What's in this?"
          It's salad.

                    REX
               (gasping)
          With ... with ... onions?

                    BREE
          What?

182

Rex tries to STAND. He is unable to
BREATHE.

>   REX
>   (accusingly)
>   You put onions in my salad!

>   BREE
>   No, I didn't. You're allergic to ...
>   (then, horrified)
>   ... oh, wait.

Rex falls over onto the floor,
UNCONSCIOUS.

INT. MEYER HOUSE - KITCHEN - DAY

Susan and Jenna are SEATED at the
table. Long beat. Suddenly Susan
SLAMS her hand down on the table.

>   SUSAN
>   PLAY DATE!

Jenna, STARTLED, reacts.

>   JENNA
>   What?

>   SUSAN
>   You're gonna call Mike's son and ask
>   him over for a play date.

>   JENNA
>   Mom, I'm ten. I don't have play dates
>   anymore.

>   SUSAN
>   But this way Mike will have to bring
>   him over. Then while you kids are in
>   the backyard playing, we can sit in
>   the kitchen and talk. It'll be like
>   a date without the pressure.

>   JENNA
>   I want to help you out, but come on.
>   He's in kindergarten! He's a baby!

>   SUSAN
>   (begging)
>   Jenna, please. You have to call him.

>   JENNA
>   (defiantly)
>   No.

Susan examines the DETERMINATION in
Jenna's face. After a beat, she reaches
in her PURSE and pulls out a CELL
PHONE.

>   SUSAN
>   You know how I said you can't get
>   your ears pierced til you're twelve?

>   JENNA
>   (suspicious)
>   Yeah.

>   SUSAN
>   How'd you like to get 'em pierced
>   this Saturday?

Susan confidently HANDS her daughter
the CELL PHONE. After a beat, Jenna
takes the phone and begins DIALING.

INT. SCAVO HOUSE - KITCHEN - DAY

Lynette is SEATED at the kitchen table.
Beside her in a high chair is her
TODDLER. Lynette is holding a jar of
BABY FOOD and a SPOON. The toddler is
SCREAMING.

>   LYNETTE
>   (begging)
>   Sweetie, I know you want Mommy's
>   milk, but Mommy's breasts can't take
>   it anymore. I need you to eat your
>   num num peaches. What do you say?

Lynette's toddler throws a handful of
PEACHES in Lynette's FACE. A look of
utter DEFEAT crosses Lynette's face.

>   PETER/PAUL/PRESTON (O.S.)
>   Mommy!! Mommy!!

>   LYNETTE
>   (calling out)
>   Now what is it?

Peter comes rushing in.

>   PETER
>   Daddy's home!

>   LYNETTE
>   What?

Peter and Lynette RUSH out of the
kitchen into the living room. Lynette
RUSHES back in, PICKS UP her toddler
and RUSHES back out again.

INT. SCAVO HOUSE - LIVING ROOM -
CONTINUOUS

Lynette rushes in just as TOM enters
the front door. He is carrying a
SUITCASE and a SHOPPING BAG. Peter,

MC: In this draft there
were no mystery agendas
with Mike. He was just a
nice, normal guy. The
whole comedy was based
on the idea that Susan was
making her daughter play
with this young boy so she
would have a moment
alone with Mike. And I
realized it was also better
that he didn't have a kid,
because of his secret
agenda coming there.

183

Paul, and Preston IMMEDIATELY rush to his side and HUG him.

PETER/PAUL/PRESTON
Daddy!!!

TOM
Hey, boys! Hey, honey.

LYNETTE
Tom, I wasn't expecting you for another week.

TOM
I'm just here for the night. I'm going to Frisco in the morning.

PRESTON
Daddy, did you bring us presents?

TOM
I don't know. Let's see.

Tom reaches into the SHOPPING BAG. He pulls out a FOOTBALL.

PETER/PAUL/PRESTON
A football!!

TOM
But I'm not gonna give it to you unless you promise to go outside right now and practice throwing for twenty minutes. Will you promise?

PETER/PAUL/PRESTON
We promise!

Tom hands the boys the FOOTBALL and they go RUSHING outside.

LYNETTE
Honey, I'm so glad you're back. Even if it's for one night.

TOM
I know. I've missed you, too.

They kiss PASSIONATELY, trying to maneuver around the BABY in Lynette's arms. Tom suddenly takes PATSY out of Lynette's arms and places her in the CRIB.

TOM
Here. Come with me.

Tom PULLS Lynette into the BEDROOM.

INT. SCAVO HOUSE - BEDROOM - CONTINUOUS

DOUG SAVANT: In the pilot there was only one scene between Lynette and Tom. She was a desperate housewife and I was just a husband. I had no idea what the writers had planned for us. But Felicity was always generous and inclusive, and for that coming home scene, we successfully overcame the awkwardness of being thrown into a physical relationship immediately. After we had shot the pilot I saw her at a party for an ABC show and she said hi. I said, "I liked our stuff." She said, "So did I." It gave me a sense that we were going to be okay.

Tom immediately starts TAKING off Lynette's CLOTHES.

LYNETTE
You want to have sex? Tom, I look awful. And I'm exhausted.

TOM
Sorry, baby. But I gotta have it.

LYNETTE
Is it okay if I just sorta lay there?

TOM
Absolutely.

Tom lays Lynette down on the BED. He RIPS off his shirt and pants and then LAYS on top of Lynette and begins KISSING her. After a beat Lynette begins EAGERLY kissing him back.

LYNETTE
God, I love you.

TOM
I love you more.

Tom begins undoing the BUTTONS on Lynette's BLOUSE. She suddenly PULLS away.

LYNETTE
Wait. I gotta tell you. I was having problems with swelling so the doctor took me off the pill. You'll have to put on a condom.

TOM
(annoyed)
A condom?
(then)
Oh, what the heck. Let's risk it.

Lynette stares in DISBELIEF at Tom's SMILING face.

She then REARS back and PUNCHES him in the face, sending Tom REELING. She grabs her CLOTHES and EXITS, leaving a stunned Tom clutching his face in PAIN.

INT. SOLIS HOUSE - BEDROOM - AFTERNOON

Gabrielle and John are LYING quietly and contentedly in bed. They are each lost in their own THOUGHTS. Gabrielle looks over at a PICTURE she has on her nightstand.

GABRIELLE'S POV: A snapshot of Gabrielle, Lynette, Susan, Bree, and

Mary Alice at a picnic all LAUGHING together.

Gabrielle looks at the picture SADLY. John sees that she's DISTRACTED by something.

> JOHN
> What are you thinking about?

> GABRIELLE
> Nothing.

> JOHN
> Come on. Tell me.

> GABRIELLE
> I was thinking about my friend, Mary Alice.

> JOHN
> And ... ?

> GABRIELLE
> ... and how lucky I am to have a gardener.

Gabrielle turns and KISSES John. They passionately embrace.

> JOHN
> By the way, the yard looks great.

> GABRIELLE
> Thanks.

They continue KISSING. Suddenly:

> CARLOS (O.S.)
> Gaby, I'm home.

Gaby and John BOLT upright.

> JOHN
> What the hell ... ?!

> GABRIELLE
> The window!!

They both JUMP out of the bed and begin FRANTICALLY searching for their clothes. Gabrielle slips on an oversized T-SHIRT.

> CARLOS (O.S.)
> Gaby! Where are you?

> JOHN
> I can't find my clothes!

> GABRIELLE
> Leave 'em!

Gabrielle SLIDES open the window, GRABS the NAKED JOHN and pushes him OUT. She then RIPS all the BEDDING off the bed. She finds John's CLOTHES tangled in the sheets. Just then, the DOOR opens. She quickly SHOVES the clothes under the BED.

Carlos ENTERS.

> CARLOS
> Well, there you are!

> GABRIELLE
> (calmly)
> Carlos, what a surprise. What are you doing home in the middle of the day?

> CARLOS
> (tears in his eyes)
> I closed the deal with Tanaka! Can you believe it? We gotta celebrate!!!

Carlos HUGS Gabrielle.

> GABRIELLE
> Great. Can you give me a second?
> (off bedding)
> I was getting ready to do laundry.

> CARLOS
> Sure. Oh, hi, John.

A look of PANIC passes over Gabrielle's face. She turns to see that JOHN, whose bare chest is VISIBLE from the waist up, is standing outside the bedroom window. He is holding PRUNING SHEARS and is CLIPPING the hedge outside the window.

> JOHN
> (nonchalantly)
> Hey, Mr. Solis. Hey, Mrs. Solis.

Gabrielle NERVOUSLY looks from John to Carlos, WAITING to see what will HAPPEN next.

> JOHN
> Mr. Solis, if you meet me in the front, I'll show you where I'm gonna plant the hydrangeas.

> CARLOS
> Be there in a second.
> (then, to Gabrielle)
> Baby, we're gonna make so much money off this deal. Are you happy for me?

GABRIELLE
I'm happy for us both.

Carlos EXITS. Gabrielle looks over
JOHN, who is still at the window,
wearing nothing but a COCKY grin.

EXT. HUBER HOUSE - BACKYARD -
CONTINUOUS

Mrs. Huber is on a LADDER picking fruit
off a TREE. As she mounts a higher
RUNG of the ladder, she casually LOOKS
over into the Solis backyard and sees
the NAKED backside of JOHN, who is
still peering into Gabrielle's BEDROOM
window.

Mrs. Huber FALLS off her ladder.

INT. HOSPITAL ROOM - NIGHT

Rex is lying awake in a BED. Bree is in
a chair by his side. There is SILENCE.
Then:

REX
I can't believe you tried to kill me.

BREE
Yes, well, I feel badly about that.

REX
(pointedly)
Do you?

BREE
I told you it was a mistake. Evie
came over and I was distracted ...

REX
Since when do you make mistakes?

BREE
What is that supposed to mean?

REX
You're always so perfect. Never a
hair out of place. Never a false
move. You're this perfect suburban
housewife with her pearls and her
spatula who says things like "We owe
the Hendersons a dinner." Jesus,
Bree, where is the woman I fell in
love with, who used to burn the toast
and drink milk out of the carton?
And laugh. I need her. Not this
cold, perfect thing you've become.

BREE
(hurt)
Rex ...

REX
Flaws are messy things. Maybe in a
fit of cleaning, you just got rid of
yours.

Bree STARES at Rex for a moment. She is
DEVASTATED. Then, with all the DIGNITY
she can MUSTER, Bree walks over and
PICKS UP a vase of FLOWERS off the table
next to Rex.

BREE
(simply)
These need water.

Bree CROSSES into the bathroom.

INT. HOSPITAL BATHROOM - CONTINUOUS

Bree shuts the door. She goes to the
sink and begins to FILL the vase up
with WATER. She looks up and SEES
herself in the MIRROR. She begins to
SOB. She quickly puts her HAND over
her mouth to MUFFLE the sound.

MARY ALICE (V.O.)
Bree sobbed quietly in the restroom
for twenty minutes. But her husband
never knew. Because when Bree
finally emerged ...

INT. HOSPITAL ROOM - A LITTLE LATER

Bree EMERGES from the bathroom looked
as POISED and as COLLECTED as she did
going in.

MARY ALICE (V.O.)
... she was perfect.

INT. MEYER HOUSE - LIVING ROOM - DAY

SUSAN and JENNA open the door to reveal
MIKE.

SUSAN
Hey, Mike. Thanks for coming over.
This is my daughter, Jenna.

MIKE
Nice to meet you. This is my son,
Timmy.

TIMMY
(shyly)
Hello.

Jenna, APPALLED, looks up at her
mother. Susan SUBTLY touches her
earlobes. Jenna immediately gets her
MEANING.

MC: I loved this moment where John goes out the window, which we ultimately used in Episode 101. We got rid of it here because we needed the lawnmower scene to be the climax of Gabrielle's story. Instead we added the quiet scene with Gabrielle and John talking, which was important for her character.

STEVEN CULP: In the middle of my first audition, I was reading the scene in the hospital where Rex says he wants the woman he married. I got to a particular point in the scene and I just felt confused. I wasn't sure it was supposed to be funny or serious. When I realized I wasn't going to get back in the moment, I said, "I'm going to stop now. Thank you." I left and I went home, feeling sheepish. The next day, my manager called and said, "What happened at *Desperate Housewives?*" I told her what happened and she said, "That's interesting because they loved you and they want to see you again today and I think you might get an offer on this." I realized that all those things I was feeling were appropriate for the character. When I went back in I thought, *I'm not going to worry about getting this job or impressing them or impressing me. I just want to find out where this thing is going to lead me.* And it went very well.

JENNA
(resigned)
Come on, Timmy. Backyard's this way.

INT. MEYER HOUSE - KITCHEN - A LITTLE
LATER

Susan and Mike are SEATED at the table,
LAUGHING.

SUSAN
... and I always thought of myself
as this capable feminist. I divorce
Karl and suddenly I'm like, "Crap.
Who's gonna kill the spiders?"

MIKE
Hey, I never learned to cook. The
day after Amy's funeral, I tried
to fix waffles for breakfast. Timmy
took one bite and said, "Daddy, for
what it's worth, I know how to make
cereal."

They continue LAUGHING. Then:

SUSAN
You seem like you've adjusted to the
whole single parent thing pretty
well.

MIKE
I'm trying. But it's so hard. There
are days I'm juggling so much, I
don't even have time to think.

SUSAN
Yeah.
(then)
I sometimes wonder if that's what
happened to Mary Alice.

MIKE
The woman who died?

SUSAN
It's so easy to get caught up in the
day-to-day of it all. Cooking and
cleaning and carpools. We forget to
look at the big picture. And I think
maybe that's what happened to Mary
Alice. One afternoon she just ran
out of things to do. And she finally
had time to think about her life.
And she couldn't remember what she
was doing it all for. And in that
awful, awful moment, she decided ...

Susan stops. Then:

MIKE
That's the trick, isn't it? To
remember what we're doing it for.

They SIT for a beat contemplating
this. Suddenly they HEAR the sound of
children's LAUGHTER. A knowing GRIN
spreads across both their faces. They
get up and go to the kitchen window.

MIKE AND SUSAN'S POV: Jenna and Timmy
are RUNNING around PLAYING. They
genuinely seem to be having a good
time.

Mike and Susan continue WATCHING their
children, enjoying the scene. Susan
turns and LOOKS up at Mike. He RETURNS
her gaze. They SMILE at each other.

As they look into each other's eyes,
they realize there is a CONNECTION
here.

Mike suddenly LEANS in and KISSES
Susan. He PULLS BACK instantly,
waiting to see if he did the right
thing.

Susan, who's in SHOCK, looks at him for
a BEAT, then lunges for him. She GRABS
his head with her hands and PULLS him
back toward her. They begin kissing
PASSIONATELY. Suddenly Jenna opens the
sliding SCREEN DOOR. Timmy is beside
her.

JENNA
Mom?

Susan and Mike immediately PUSH away
from each other. Mike GRABS a paper
off the table and STARTS to read it.
Susan goes to the PANTRY and PRETENDS
to look for something.

SUSAN
(nonchalantly)
Yes, Jenna.

JENNA
Timmy wanted a glass of water.
(sensing something's wrong)
Is that okay?

SUSAN
Sure. That's fine.

Jenna and Timmy step INSIDE. Susan
CROSSES to the sink. As she FILLS a
glass with water, she GLANCES back at
Mike.

Mike SMILES at her KNOWINGLY. Susan SMILES back.

<u>EXT. MEYER HOUSE - FRONT YARD - A LITTLE WHILE LATER</u>

Everyone is at the FRONT DOOR saying good-bye.

> MIKE
> ... thanks again for having us over.

> SUSAN
> It was our pleasure. Anytime.

Mike and Timmy START to exit. Mike turns BACK.

> MIKE
> Can I ... call you later?

> SUSAN
> I'd like that.

Mike smiles. He and Timmy EXIT. Susan SHUTS the door. Jenna WHIRLS her MOTHER around.

> JENNA
> So tell me! How did it go?

> SUSAN
> (contentedly)
> It was nice. It was very nice.

> JENNA
> That's it? I played three hours of Hide-and-Go-Seek for "nice?"

EXASPERATED, Jenna exits to her bedroom. Susan WALKS into the kitchen, lost in her THOUGHTS.

> MARY ALICE (V.O.)
> Normally, Susan would have told her daughter all that had transpired. But she was quietly thrilled to finally have a secret. A secret she wasn't ready share. The secret that she was in love with the plumber who lived across the street.

As she pours herself a cup of coffee, Susan SMILES.

<u>INT. SCOTT HOUSE - BEDROOM - DAY</u>

Various DRESSES and ACCESSORIES are strewn about the room. The four women are PACKING them all into BOXES.

> MARY ALICE (V.O.)
> The next day my friends came together to help empty out my closets. All of them still grieving for me. Albeit, in their own special way.

Lynette PICKS UP a dress and EXAMINES the tag.

> LYNETTE
> Aha! Mary Alice was a size eight! For years she told me she was a size six. Finally, I have proof!

> SUSAN
> Lynnie, after you die, do you want us checking out your dress sizes?

> LYNETTE
> There's no need for threats.

Lynette TOSSES the dress in a box. Gabrielle picks up a BLOUSE.

> GABRIELLE
> Oh, now this is gorgeous. Mary Alice should have been buried in this.

Susan looks at the BLOUSE.

> SUSAN
> You think that's gorgeous?

> GABRIELLE
> Yes, I do.

Gabrielle crosses the room and STUFFS the blouse into a BOX. Susan turns to Lynette.

> SUSAN
> When my time is up, under no circumstances is Gabrielle allowed to dress my corpse.

> GABRIELLE
> (turning around)
> I heard that.

Susan REACTS. Bree, who's finished TAPING up a box, STANDS.

> BREE
> All right, guys. Let's get these boxes outside. I want to make it to Goodwill before three.

<u>EXT. SCOTT HOUSE - FRONT YARD - CONTINUOUS</u>

The WOMEN all emerge, each carrying a BOX.

> LYNETTE
> Size eight. Poor Mary Alice. I guess that was the skeleton in her closet.

> MARY ALICE (V.O.)
> Not quite, Lynette. Not quite.

Suddenly a COAT falls out of the BOX Susan is CARRYING. When she BENDS over to PICK it up, she sees a LETTER, stuffed in one of the POCKETS. Susan PULLS the letter out.

> GABRIELLE
> What's that, Susan?

> SUSAN
> It's some kind of letter. It's addressed to Mary Alice.

> MARY ALICE (V.O.)
> How ironic. To have something I tried so desperately to keep secret, treated so casually ...

Susan starts to OPEN the letter.

> BREE
> You shouldn't read that, Susan. It's private.

> LYNETTE
> It looks like it's already been opened. What the big deal?

> MARY ALICE (V.O.)
> But keeping secrets is hard. And keeping them from your friends is even harder.

Susan opens the letter. The girls READ over her shoulder.

> MARY ALICE (V.O.)
> I'm so sorry, girls. I never wanted you to be burdened with this. I really didn't.

Susan UNFOLDS the letter. All the women READ it together.

THE WOMEN'S P.O.V.: A slightly crumpled note that read:

I KNOW WHAT YOU DID. IT MAKES ME SICK.
AND I'M GONNA TELL.

The note is unsigned. The women stare at it in STUNNED silence. Then:

> LYNETTE
> The postmark. Look at the postmark.

> BREE
> She must have gotten this the day she died.

> GABRIELLE
> Omigod. Do you think this is the reason she ... ?

Even though Gabrielle STOPS, everyone knows what she was about to say. The same HORRIBLE thought is OCCURRING to all of them. Finally:

> SUSAN
> (whispering)
> Oh, Mary Alice. What did you do?

The four women remain FROZEN on the front LAWN as the camera pulls back. We see a man JOG by. Two girls are jumping rope. The camera pulls back even farther to show another man is MOWING his lawn. Cars are PASSING. It's a beautiful day in SUBURBIA.

And nobody seems to be DESPERATE.

FADE OUT

ACKNOWLEDGEMENTS

I would love to acknowledge the stars of my show, my writing staff, my directors, and my crew who made the show possible. This book wouldn't have been possible if they hadn't done such an amazing job this season.

I'd also love to thank all the folks at Hyperion Publishing and my agents, Andy and Debbee, who assured me if we did a book like this, it would be classy. Thank God they were right.

Lastly I'd love to acknowledge Amy. For obvious reasons. You're the best, hon. —Marc Cherry

ABOUT THE CONTRIBUTORS

This book was produced by Downtown Bookworks Inc., a New York–based book packager with extensive experience in media tie-ins.

PRESIDENT

Julie Merberg

DIRECTOR

Patty Brown

EDITOR

Sara Newberry

Downtown Bookworks Inc.
285 West Broadway, New York, NY 10013

This book was designed by Number Seventeen, a New York–based, award-winning, multi-disciplinary design firm working in print, film, and television.

CREATIVE DIRECTION

Emily Oberman & Bonnie Siegler

DESIGN

Wade Convay

Number Seventeen
285 West Broadway, New York, NY 10013

HYPERION, TOUCHSTONE TELEVISION AND ABC GIVE SPECIAL THANKS TO:

Bob Miller
Ellen Archer
Will Schwalbe
Gretchen Young
Zareen Jaffery
Linda Prather
Dan Taylor
Deirdre Smerillo
Bruce Gersh
Melissa Harling
Mark Pedowitz
Yana Matlof
Dan Richards
Jason Hoffman

And to all the *Desperate Housewives* production staff who were so helpful and gave their time

CREDITS

PAGES 90—91

PAGES 92—93

PAGES 152—155

MARC CHERRY GOT THE NAME "WISTERIA LANE" FROM *THE BOOK OF LISTS*, WHICH HAD A LIST OF THE MOST BEAUTIFUL WORDS IN THE ENGLISH LANGUAGE, AND *WISTERIA* WAS ONE OF THEM. LATER, AFTER THE SHOW WAS PICKED UP, CHERRY LEARNED THAT THE WISTERIA VINE IS A VERY DESTRUCTIVE PLANT THAT CRUSHES OTHERS AS IT GROWS.

DESPERATE HOUSEWIVES

Printed in the United States of America.

For information address Hyperion,
77 West 66th Street, New York, New York
10023-6298.

Library of Congress
Cataloging-in-Publication Data

ISBN: 1-4013-0826-0

Hyperion books are available for special promotions and premiums.

For details contact Michael Rentas,
Assistant Director, Inventory Operations,
Hyperion, 77 West 66th Street, 11th floor,
New York, New York 10023, or
call 212-456-0133.

10 9 8 7 6 5 4 3 2 1

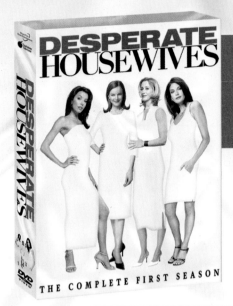

Uncover even more secrets of Wisteria Lane with over five hours of revealing bonus features—*Desperate Housewives: The Complete First Season.* **Now On DVD.**

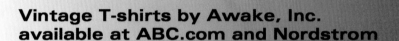

Vintage T-shirts by Awake, Inc. available at ABC.com and Nordstrom

Now fans of *Desperate Housewives* can enjoy their favorite show with the *Desperate Housewives 2006 Calendar,* featuring full-color images from the show and quotes from America's favorite housewives.

Welcome to Wisteria Lane!—In the *Desperate Housewives Dirty Laundry Game* each player has something to hide. Try not to let your secret out! Available everywhere games are sold.

Cardinal®

Watch *Desperate Housewives* Sundays on abc

Desperate Housewives © 2005 Touchstone Television. All Rights Reserved.